ENERGY AND PERSONAL POWER

Other Books by Shirley Gehrke Luthman:

Intimacy: The Essence of Male and Female
Collections 1979
Available through:
Mehetabel & Co.
4340 Redwood Highway, Suite 307
San Rafael, CA 94903

The Dynamic Family
Available through:
Science and Behavior Books
P.O. Box 11457
Palo Alto, CA 94306

Energy
and
Personal Power

Shirley Gehrke Luthman

MEHETABEL & CO.
SAN RAFAEL, CALIFORNIA

Printed in the United States of America
Cover and Book Design by Mary Russel, Sausalito, CA

First printing, June 1982

For information contact the publisher:
Mehetabel & Company
4340 Redwood Highway, Suite 307
San Rafael, Ca 94903

Dedicated to
Three Pioneer Women

To my Mother, Velma Jones Gehrke, who has always faced life with unbounded, exuberant energy.

To my Grandmother, Pearl Jones, whose indomitable spirit and strength set an example for me.

To my Aunt, Evelyn Jones Hays, whose sensitivity and intuitive awareness strengthened my own.

Acknowledgments

I want to express special appreciation to my friend, Carmen Lynch, who was instrumental in supporting me in the development of these concepts and of my own expanding awareness.

Thanks also to the members of my original study group: Pamela Blum, Paula Bottome, Al Carr, Ilene Dillon, Tom Dunn, Ernest Hall, John and Nancy Jungerman, Werner Kuhne, and Carmen Lynch.

Table of Contents

1
By Way of Introduction

"If on your way you meet the Buddha, kill him...O
disciples of the truth, make an effort to free yourselves from
every object...O you, with eyes of moles! I say to you:
No Buddha, no teaching, no discipline! What are you
ceaselessly looking for in your neighbor's house? Don't you
understand that you are putting a head higher than your
own? What then is lacking to you in yourselves? That which
you have at this moment does not differ from that of which
the Buddha is made."*

I HAVE HAD GREAT DIFFICULTY in giving up both my own image of
myself as teacher and expert, and my search for others who could
be gurus for me. I have been a therapist for twenty years and a teacher-
consultant to others in the helping professions for more than ten years.
It became apparent to me that I had a secret pact with my clients
and students. In return for their adulation and obeisance—only what
any goddess would deserve—I would be always giving, understanding, unruffled, and have all the answers. The price we each paid for
this arrangement was heavy. I felt isolated in my ivory tower, frequently drained emotionally, and experienced that I was spending a good
deal of my time doing things that did not bring me joy. The reci-
pients of my expertise developed a kind of dependency on me in which
they trusted my judgments, my perceptions, my directions more than
their own. I became the model of perfection to which they ascribed—a
pedestal equally devastating to us all. All of us were constantly
depreciating ourselves by adhering to some image of what we thought
we should be or of what we thought was expected of us rather than
who we really were. We were supported in this arrangement by a

---

* *Willard and Marguerite Beecher, Beyond Success and Failure,* A quote from an old
Zen monk, Rinzai.

culture in which education is based primarily on right and wrong. The teacher ostensibly has all the answers, and the students, like baby birds, wait open-mouthed for pearls of wisdom to drop into their beaks. They are not expected to swallow or digest the largesse, only to feed it back exactly as it was presented. For this feat, they are rewarded as being right and, therefore, bright. Most of us support this one-up, one-down arrangement in our institutions and relationships because it seems to reduce our anxieties, make us feel more secure, and keep us from taking risks. It also keeps us infantile and our learning on a primitive level.

However, if we give up such an arrangement, we have to trust our intuition—that the answers we need are inside each of us. That means we have to trust our basic natures as healthy, reliable, loving, and non-destructive. A tall order for most of us. In my development, I came to the realization that the more alive, joyous, and healthy I felt, the more success I experienced in every area of my life. In addition, my ability to heal others in terms of assisting them in their growth was greatly enhanced. Therefore, perhaps I needed to take responsibility for my own aliveness. It was immediately evident to me that trying to define myself in relation to other people's expectations did not turn me on.

It is within this context that I offer this book to you. Please don't read it in terms of whether or not it is right or wrong. As you read, let the words wash over you and trigger thoughts, sensations, images, fantasies, and dreams. Trust that whatever I say that is meaningful to you, your insides will retain and use. Whatever I say that is not fitting to you, a l l ow yourself to discard easily. The end result of this process will be something new that is a synthesis of your insides and mine expressed through the channel of your unique entity. No outcome could be more desirable than that.

> "'For what do I go to this far land which no one has ever reached? Oh, I am alone! I am utterly alone!'
> And Reason, that old man, said to her, 'Silence! What do you hear?'
> And she listened intently, and she said, 'I hear a sound of feet, a thousand times ten thousand and thousand of thousands, and they beat this way!'
> He said, 'They are the feet of those that shall follow you. Lead on! Make a track to the water's edge! Where you stand

now, the ground will be beaten flat by ten thousand times ten thousand feet.' And he said, 'Have you seen the locusts how they cross a stream? First one comes down to the water-edge, and it is swept away, and then another comes and then another, and then another, and at last with their bodies piled up a bridge is built and the rest pass over.'

She said, 'And, of those that come first, some are swept away and are heard of no more; their bodies do not even build the bridge?'

'And are swept away, and are heard of no more—and what of that?' he said.

'And what of that—' she said.

'They make a track to the water's edge.'

'They make a track to the water's edge!' And she said, 'Over that bridge which shall be built with our bodies, who will pass?'

He said, 'The entire human race."

And the woman grasped her staff.

And I saw her turn down that dark path to the river."*

This beautiful passage was written by a woman who was far ahead of her time—a true explorer. Often, tears come to my eyes when I read that passage because I experience it as the soliloquy of the pioneer. I think about how many people in our history have risked themselves in uncharted seas, land, sky, and psyche and, by doing so, have paved the way for you and me. I feel that you and I have the opportunity now to pioneer in the exploration of our internal worlds via our intuition, expanded levels of consciousness, and those senses in addition to the five with which we are familiar.

So, our journey begins . . .

---

* Howard Thurman, Ed., *Track to the Water's Edge.* Originally by Olive Schreiner, *Dreams.* Boston: Little Brown and Co., 1900.

2
My Own Journey
Suffering

WHEN I WAS IN GRADUATE SCHOOL to get my MSW (Master's degree in Social Work), my training was Freudian oriented. My education about how human beings developed emotionally and about how to appropriately handle emotional problems both in myself and others came from the principles and concepts expressed by Sigmund Freud. The implication which I perceived in my education was that our potential was permanently impaired by the extent of deprivation or trauma we endured in our early life experiences. We could learn to adjust to our losses so that we might live reasonably successful, fulfilled lives, just like one can learn to live without an arm or leg or one kidney. However, though I don't remember that anyone ever actually *said* this, I came away with the conclusion that an individual could be made permanently inadequate or impaired, depending on the extent of his deprivation or trauma. Therefore, we were, in a sense, victims of whatever fate determined our parentage. Of course, some of us might initially be of more superior protoplasm than others, so there were degrees of damage. As a result of what was really quite extensive, diligent, and well-structured education in the inter and intra-personal dynamics of human development, I graduated with a superior ability to diagnose, within an inch of his life, what was wrong with an individual and how he got that way. Also, I could, and often did, write a profound treatise of the subject for the perusal of my various supervisors and instructors who were busy diagnosing me. My main preoccupation in graduate school, by way of digression, was to give my supervisors enough information about myself to keep them happy in the feeling they were assisting me, but not enough for them to find out what I was *really* like and, thus, perhaps boot me out of school as unfit to do therapy with others because I had too many problems

16

of my own. As I was unclear about what constituted such a judgment, I spent all of my graduate training walking an emotional tightrope and trying to learn something without exposing my deepest fears, doubts, and questions. I think that on some tacit level, the school system operates on the basis that if you can survive that kind of pressure, you may be less likely to fall apart in the face of a client's intense emotional trauma.

At any rate, though my diagnostic ability pleased my supervisors and gave me a sense of security, it presented one problem. Once I had someone neatly wrapped up in my diagnostic report, I didn't know what to do next. What do you do with someone whom you believe to be permanently impaired? The problem was further complicated by the fact that I never got to watch anyone else do therapy, and no one ever watched me. As a result, we were left with each other's reports of what we did, and there was no way to tell what was real and what was fantasy even if we could understand the reports. So, I learned how to do therapy primarily by doing it. Fortunately, many people feel better and enhance their growth just by ventilating their feelings and experiences to someone who listens without giving advice or judgments. Thus I was able to hold my first jobs until I gained enough confidence to begin to experiment and explore new ways of being with my clients. In addition, I worked in a variety of settings like mental hospitals, out-patient clinics, adoption agencies, welfare departments, family service agencies, and school counseling departments. Such experience gave me knowledge about a diverse selection of people from every strata of society, with information about how they coped successfully with life situations as well as how and why they developed symptoms. I feel that one of the most important advantages of being a therapist is the opportunity to learn alternative ways of looking and doing. Most of us do not share intimate feelings and experiences with friends as we would with a therapist, and so we only have our own immediate families as the basis for learning the basic facts of living. Therefore, we may only learn one or two ways of looking at and handling a particular life situation. If those ways don't happen to fit us, we are stuck. If we had many other alternative ideas based on intimate knowledge of the way others handle such situations, we would not only have more choices but more stimulation to develop unique ways of our own. This is one of the aids that clients get from therapists—a much broader base of knowledge about how other people do things.

After spending several years developing such a base of knowledge and experience, I found that my interests lay much more in the direction of assisting people to expand their potential in the development of individual creativity and satisfying relationships than in the direction of concrete services like adoption or community organization. At this point, I developed a private practice working with individuals, couples, and families who were experiencing some difficulty in individual growth or family relationships. Again, I found myself periodically stuck with people whom I could not help. While at first I consoled myself that they could not be helped because of their basic impairments or inadequacies, I became increasingly uncomfortable with that assumption. At this point, I heard about a new method of treatment called family therapy being heralded by one of its developers and mentors, the brilliant and courageous Virginia Satir. Now, family therapy was a revolutionary development in the field for two major reasons. One was that Virginia invited people to watch her work. You could actually *see* what she did and what happened when she did it. Suddenly the aura of confidentiality was exposed primarily as a cover for the therapist's anxieties about himself because, amazingly, clients often welcomed being viewed. They expressed appreciation for the additional consultation of the ten or twelve other therapists who were observing, and pleasure at being a part of their advanced training. As a result of this openness, therapists began to expose themselves more in exploring the blocks to their own growth which became apparent as they allowed themselves to be viewed in their work. Frequently, the clients with whom we have the most difficulty are experiencing difficulties similar to our own or are triggering fears and barriers in ourselves which we didn't know we had. Thus, if the therapy process is observed away from the framework of right and wrong, it becomes a learning experience for both client and therapist.

The other major contribution of family therapy was the growth model. The growth model concept offers that there is no such state as sick or well. The individual who feels that he is growing, producing, and creating in ways that are fitting to him will be symptom-free. The individual who feels that his growth is blocked in one or more areas of his life may develop symptoms physically, emotionally, behaviorally, or in his relationships. Thus, a symptom is an indication that growth is being inhibited in some area of the individual or family life. In addition, the growth model teaches that the individual is basically sound—there are no parts missing or irreparable twists in his psyche. Whatever deprivation or trauma he experienced in his development resulted in his learning ways of expressing himself and of relating to other people that did not work for him. Thus, *he* was not basically inadequate, deformed or wrong, but the processes he had learned were wrong or un-fitting. For example, if he grew up in a family in which his parents withdrew from him or beat him violently when he got angry, he developed ways of getting what he wanted without showing his anger or he withdrew so that he was not threatening to them. At a later point in his life, his process of repressing his anger in order to get along might produce serious physical difficulty in him or interfere with his being able to form close, satisfying relationships.

In another instance, a child who didn't receive love in his early years because his parents were not around or were severely disturbed might assume that he was unloved because there was something wrong with him and operate as though that was true in his own adult life. So, he could appear to be incapable of love when, in reality, he is afraid to assert and prefers to appear inadequate and crippled rather than risk exposing an inner self he believes to be bad.

Now, the growth model freed us from the tyranny of whatever fate decreed our parentage, but it was still based on something being wrong. At this point, *we* were no longer basically wrong or impaired, but our processes—the ways we used for expressing ourselves and relating to others—were wrong. They prevented us from being clear, congruent, spontaneous and assertive in the expression of our deepest feelings, which was depreciating to our self-esteem and wrought confusion in our relationships. Such a concept made it much easier for me as a person and therapist, because now there was always hope— anyone, including myself, was not basically deficient, but was capable of achieving what he wanted by breaking down the barriers in the way to his expressing his real feelings, desires, limitations and demands.

As a therapist, I could now assist people in understanding that just because their behavior might be hurtful or depreciating to others, it didn't necessarily follow that they intended to hurt. It might be that the processes they learned for expressing themselves communicated a different message than they were intending to send. Therefore, the person didn't need overhauling. His processes were the culprit and they could be unlearned, discarded, or re-vamped to express him more clearly and, therefore, more successfully.

At this point, I would like to digress to discuss how my personal development coincided with my professional growth, because the two began to come together here. My parents had a strong affiliation with a fundamental religion during my growing up experience, which I adopted for myself with great fervor. Although they were not rigid or judgmental—on the contrary, I experienced them as quite permissive people who gave me a great deal of room—the church teachings proclaimed clear-cut, rigid rules for thought and behavior. I adopted that structure because it gave me a strong sense of security and solidarity which made it possible for me to maintain my integrity and to take risks. What matter if other people didn't validate me—God did. I may have been self-righteous in my behavior, but I didn't get intruded upon. I was prepared to go anywhere and do anything because God was in charge and he was directing me. That may have absolved me from any responsibility for my fate, but it also made it possible for me to go into uncharted new experiences with a minimum of fear.

At any rate, during my young adulthood, before I connected with the family therapy model, I was living and working in California, still attaching my survival, security, and life direction to a source outside myself—the church. At that time, my parents, who lived in Missouri, came to California to visit me and became well acqauinted with the minister of my church while there. He subsequently invited my father to come to California and work for him within the structure of the church organization. The decision was a difficult one for my parents because it involved an early retirement for my father from a position he had held for thirty years, resulting in a fifty percent cut in his retirement benefits. They finally decided to come, believing it was "God's will." The experience was a devastating, humiliating, and expensive one. They stayed a year and a half and then returned to St. Louis. At the point where the situation was at its worst and they made the decision they would have to leave, I developed what was diagnosed as a slipped disc in my back which literally immobilized me for three weeks and required about three months to heal totally. I mention all of this because, as I look back, I feel that this was the point at which my reliance on a structure outside of myself was shattered. Literally, the backbone of the structure around which I had defined myself was broken. We had done all the right things and still disaster struck. I realized that my interpretation of what God and the church were all about was erroneous.

After my parents left, I was in a state of confusion and chaos inside, and, in that state, I was open to a whole new way of looking at myself and the world around me. In that open, vulnerable state, I connected with the philosophy of the growth model—a non-judgmental approach to life based on the concept of what is fitting to the growth of the individual rather than what is right or wrong. All of the answers I had once accepted with blind faith were now open to question. In one fell swoop, I went from a closed position in which everything was clear and certain to a state in which nothing was sure. I can only surmise that I must have been in a hurry and that only a "blockbuster" experience would have shaken me loose from the rigid foundations in which I had been firmly entrenched.

I entered then into one of the most expansive personal growth periods of my life up to that point. I met and married my husband; I started the Family Therapy Institute with Dr. Martin Kirschenbaum; I went from an existence in which I could get everything I owned into the back seat of my car to one in which I was involved with a husband, step-daughter, house, dog, and a thriving business. My relationship with my husband, Merrill, gave me the most powerful impetus to my life's journey. He was a man teeming with an unbounded zest for life, and he was, at all times, totally himself. We reached a depth in our relationship that I had never before experienced. Then disaster struck again. Merrill developed a heart condition and died suddenly. I came as close to suicide as it is possible to come without taking the step. We were so inextricably bound in terms of what we had experienced together that it was as though someone had ripped out an internal gossamer web and left dangling threads, emptiness, and deadness.

With Merrill's death, the last of my own structure was demolished.

What was begun with the painful experience with my parents was finished with my loss of him. Ambition, putting off current pleasure for future gain, anything that smacked of living in the future was suddenly ludicrous. The only thing that had any meaning was feeling totally alive in the now. It took me a year to let go of him and to come back to life. A year and a half after Merrill died, my father died. My mother came out to California, and, in addition to my own pain, I watched her go through what I had experienced the previous year. I began to feel as though I was immersed in death. During that time, I threw myself into my work and into the development of the Institute. Dr. Kirschenbaum and I were beginning to develop a reputation for our innovative work in doing and teaching family therapy. We were invited to teach and consult with professionals all over the United States, Canada, and in Europe. The pressure on us became tremendous. We were traveling, carrying on an extensive training program at the Institute, seeing clients, administering research programs and a staff of ten, including two secretaries and eight other therapists who were then employed by us.

At this point, I again had a physical set-back. I developed a serious internal infection that was excruciatingly painful. It was cured within three weeks, but it left me weakened and exhausted, and it made me stop and take notice. Why should I become ill? I was working very hard, but I also made a point of taking good care of myself—getting enough sleep, eating well, exercising and including a fair amoung of play-time. As I took stock, I realized that I was spending much of my time driving myself, doing a lot of things that I enjoyed once I got into them, but that I had to push myself to start. I also realized that I had always wanted to write, but that I had been telling myself that I would do it when I got everything else organized so that I had enough money to begin to decrease my work load. Only that never seemed to happen. I decided that my body was trying to tell me something and set about arranging to cut back drastically in my schedule so that I would have time to write. To do this required an emotional letting-go—I had to let go of my fear that I would lose something by passing up opportunities to make money, garner prestige, make a contribution, and even just to hang on to what I had, by taking time for myself to do what I really wanted to do. It was another step in my letting go of controlling my environment so that I would feel safe and secure at the cost of diminishing my experience of joy and aliveness in the moment.

During that year in which I arranged for a reduced schedule, I wrote my first book.* The writing of that book was an intense emotional experience for me. There were times when I felt as though I was pulling the words out of quicksand or molasses, and other times when they seemed to flow through me from the air around and I wept as I wrote or felt a thrill of awe and excitement. I dedicated the book to my husband and my father, and I realized that it represented a final goodbye—an end to that part of my life dominated by my experiences with each of them. I finished the book in September of 1971, and it was published in November of 1972. In September of 1972, I resumed my schedule at the Institute, but with some modifications so that it was not so heavy as before. I was also more trusting of myself in a new way. I had said I was going to write a book, and I had done it—with no assurance it was possible beside something deep inside of me that said it was time.

---

* Shirley Gehrke Luthman, *Intimacy—The Essence of Male and Female.* Mehetabel & Company.

3
My Own Journey Awakening

AROUND THIS TIME, I had another experience which catapulted me into still a deeper level of awareness about myself. Following my husband's death, I frequently found myself in an extremely depressed state emotionally, based on my sense of loss and helplessness at the blow I thought fate had dealt me. The depressions did not hamper my life activities in any particular way nor do I think others were particularly aware of them. I saved them for time alone with myself when I could wallow in self-pity and helpless anger at the loneliness I was experiencing in comparison with what I had had. During the time I was writing, these depressions disappeared, but when the book was finished they returned with vengeance. I remember frequently thinking that if things didn't shift in a better direction or if they got too unbearable, I could always do away with myself, and that thought would comfort me. It wasn't as though I was actually planning such a step. It was more that death was my ace in the hole, my final revenge on a life that seemed meaningless and quietly desperate.

At the worst of this period, I had an automobile accident. A child on a bicycle came shooting down a sloping driveway and shot diagonally in front of my car so that we collided. The experience was striking in two ways. First, I felt there was no way I could have avoided that accident except by not being in that place at that time. Second, when I watched, horrified, as that child was thrown over the hood of my car and onto the ground, I was aware of two distinct perceptions. It was as though some deep part of me was speaking to my cognitive level. One message was, "He is not going to die," and the other was, "I've had enough! You can no longer exist holding on to both life and death like some recalcitrant child who will not play unless everything is going her way. In order to experience life fully alive, you must commit to life all the way, with no conditions."

At that point, I made that commitment. I don't mean to imply that that child's health was momentarily impaired to teach me something. I think the experience may have involved some learning for him also in terms of taking responsibility for his own safety. Perhaps that was the only way he would learn, and, if so, it may have protected him from future permanent injury or damage. At any rate, I feel that his learning process and mine connected at that point in time to teach us each whatever we needed to know.

With that commitment to life and aliveness, no matter what the risk, and the subsequent gradual diminution of my depressions, I decided I needed time to take stock of where I was in my life, what I really wanted, and where I wanted to go. For that purpose, I arranged a seven month sabbatical beginning in February of 1973. I knew I wanted to write another book to pull together all the concepts, training methods, and treatment techniques my partner and I had developed in our eight years of working together. However, I felt that would only take three or four months. I knew I needed the rest of the time for myself, but I hadn't the slightest idea how I would use it.

Following the infection I had had a few years before, I had begun to experiment with the use of vitamins and food supplements on the assumption that perhaps my diet, while balanced, wasn't sufficient to meet my needs, particularly in view of the pace I maintained and the stress under which I was operating. One thing led to another and I found myself gradually changing my dietary habits to exclude sugar, white flour and coffee from my diet almost totally; to include foods new to me like honey, wheat germ and Adele Davis' Pep-Up drink and, to greatly increase my intake of raw fruits and vegetables. I had been taking three thyroid grains a day for ten years, not because my throid was measurably deficient, but because my own thyroid hormone didn't seem to function as efficiently for me as the artificial one. I experimented with large does of vitamin B and sea kelp (iodine) and was able to discontinue the thyroid extract. My thyroid functioning shifted to a measurably more efficient production than I had ever experienced. With increased efficiency of body functioning, I found that my body was much more sensitive to whatever I put into it. I began to realize that many of the foods I had previously eaten had the effect of deadening the body, as experienced by a feeling of heaviness, lethargy or dullness.

At about the same time, I also began to experiment with meditation. Some of my professional associates had recommended it as a means of expanding one's intuitive levels and sharpening sensitivity, physically and emotionally. With the meditation and the dietary changes, I found myself moving into a more disciplined exercise program of jogging and swimming. It was as though my internal energy was expanding faster than my physical body could handle it, and the exercise seemed to restore some kind of balance. None of these innovations came about because of any directive I gave myself. They all evolved as the result of some kind of inner natural flow with which I was becoming increasingly familiar.

When I began my sabbatical, all of the various aspects of my growth began to come together for me. For one thing, I didn't have to adhere to some kind of external structure. There was no need to be at a certain place at a certain time to do anything. I was completely free for the first time in my adult life to structure my life according to what I felt with no consistent demands from the outside. As a result, I learned about my natural rhythm for eating, sleeping, writing, reading, exercising, meditation, being with other people and being alone. At this point, people began turning me on to books that had to do with metaphysics, philosophy, healing, nutrition, parapsychology and religion. The first and most important of these in terms of my process was a book called *Seth Speaks*. It was recommended to me during a casual conversation with a beauty operator at a shop where I had gone for my regular trim. Other books emerged for me by equally circuitous and seemingly haphazard routes, each at a particular point when I needed it or was most ready to entertain its ideas.

For example, early in my sabbatical period, I again developed a back pain, not nearly as severe or immobilizing as my first experience, but annoying and uncomfortable. One day when I was meditating, a verse from the Bible seemed to leap out at me, "This kind goeth not out except by prayer and fasting." It happened that I had picked up two books the week before—one with a detailed chapter about fasting and how to use it effectively for healing, and the other about meditation exercises that one could use for spiritual healing or "mind treatments." I found in my explorations that most of the literature was divided into two schools of thought. One adhered to the concept of a Deity who was not an entity outside of ourselves, but with whom we were one and who could be reached by looking deep inside of ourselves and trusting our intuitive perceptions and impulses. The other did not recognize a Deity, but was based on the concept that we are one on an energy or consciousness level with all around us, animate or inanimate, and that the process of meditation put us in touch with that experience of oneness and resulted in a sense of peace and joy as we become aware of the rhythmic flow of the universal consciousness. However, it seemed to me that the basic principles of metaphysics in terms of energy flow and expanded consciousness could be applied to either framework without any difficulty, so the individual was free to move in this direction without having to subscribe to a particular system of belief.

The idea of fasting was foreign to me. I had heard of it, but ascribed it to the peculiar habits of a race in another time and place. I'm sure that at any previous time of my life, I would have been totally closed to the idea. However, at this point, I was open to almost anything, so I decided to experiment according to the rules for fasting set down in the book I had found.* The experience was a truly enlightening one to me. I did three seven day fasts over an eight month period at roughly two to three month intervals. According to Dr. Garten, fasting accomplishes three things. It cleanses the system of stored poisons; it re-establishes the body's natural metabolic balance; and, it stimulates a process in which the body feeds on its own fat and imperfect tissue first. Therefore, weight is lost in places where it is most necessary, and the body does not get that drawn look from loss of protein which some diets stimulate. My experience seemed to validate all three premises. During my first fast, I experienced an almost total lethargy and a slight headache the first three days, which Dr. Garten indicates is due to the sudden release of poisons in the system when there is no food intake. The second fast produced similar symptoms, but they were milder and only lasted one day. By the third fast, I felt fine the entire time, so the effect for me seems to be accumulative. Each successive experience seemed easier and more beneficial.

In terms of the metabolic balance, I noticed that with each fast

---

* M.L. Garten, D.C., *The Health Secrets of a Naturopathic Doctor*. Parker.

my food cravings changed. Gooey desserts became impossible for me to swallow in any extensive amount. While they still looked good, I found that a small amount once in awhile would satisfy me. My use of salt diminished without my being aware of it until it dawned on me one day that I never put it on the table anymore. I became increasingly cognizant of the more subtle flavors of foods and began to use herbs extensively instead of condiments. My tolerance for coffee diminished drastically. I experienced it like a jolt to my system. I began to crave fruits, vegetables, and milk as I had once craved breads, gravies, and pastry. All of this evolved gradually without my having to discipline, deny, or force myself, and it occurred almost out of my awareness. I realized the differences in my diet and food cravings primarily by looking back and comparing what I used to eat with what I was currently eating, without being aware of any effort to change in the moment.

In relation to the third process he mentioned, I was surprised that my face did not get a drawn or hollow look during the fast. On the contrary, to my continued surprise, people kept telling me how well I looked and asking what I was doing. Over time, I noticed a subtle re-alignment of by body structure giving me a leaner, more elongated look. I have since learned from a surgeon friend of mine that recent medical research studies have confirmed that fasting does dissolve cholesterol and calcium deposits in the arteries.

The most surprising aspect of this whole experience for me was the sense of well-being and exhilaration I felt. I did not once feel as though I was depriving or punishing myself as I had in the past when I had periodically dieted to lose a few pounds. I felt as though I was doing exactly what fit for me to do at that point in time, and there was no effort involved. The first two days, I felt hunger but no compulsion to eat. After that, I wasn't even hungry. By the third fasting period, I experienced great energy and aliveness as though every fiber of me was alert and sensitive, like antennae. Because of this energy phenomena, I am convinced that no one can force himself to fast (except by putting himself in a hospital, jail, or wiring his jaws shut) unless the experience fits his particular growth process at a given point in time. It must occur in balance with every other aspect of his being. I will explain this in detail in a later chapter.

In addition to the fasting, meditation, vitamin and food supplements, and dietary changes, I began to visit a chiropractor at the recommendation of a friend. The theory behind that treatment is that blood and energy cannot flow unblocked through the body unless the spine is kept mobilized. If it gets locked because of tension or injury, the vertebrae put undue pressure on the discs which degenerate and contract the openings through which the nerve endings pass, thus impeding the supply of blood to tissue and the elimination of waste. While I was indulging in all these various treatments, my back pain cleared up quickly. My subjective experience, in looking back, is that that back pain was a nudge which pushed me into experimenting with new ideas and techniques that I would not have paid attention to otherwise.

4
My Own Journey
New Life

WHILE ALL OF THIS was going on on a physical level, I was plunging into a whole new world on an emotional and spiritual level. The spearhead of that plunge was the book I mentioned earlier, *Seth Speaks.* * Some of the concepts that impressed me expressed ideas like these: We have the ability to project our thoughts outward into physical form and thus create our own reality; there is no object that was not formed by consciousness—consciousness always creates form; the responsibility for your life and your environment is your own. The most powerful concept for me was that suffering is only for the purpose of teaching us to live without suffering. That concept gave me the link between the growth model in which processes were wrong to the next model in which nothing was wrong, but everything could be interpreted as an expression of growth, without a pathological base, in terms of the makeup of the individual, his ways of operating, or anything else.

I began to realize that I had always assumed that to accept life, you also had to accept pain, problems, illness and death. Everything that goes up must come down. Suffering is normal and is to be expected. It occurred to me—what if that is not so? What if we have suffering, death, depression, and problems only because we are convinced that these states are necessary to normal life? Suppose it is possible for us to program ourselves into certain states of being and repeat the patterns continually only because we are not open to the possibility that life does not have to be this way? I began to think that it isn't even a matter of believing in or being convinced that another way of living is truer. It is simply a matter of keeping our minds open to the possibilities, because in refusing to consider other

---

* Jane Roberts, *Seth Speaks.* Bantam Books.

possibilities, we automatically close them off. For example, suppose you are convinced on the inside of yourself that you are unlovable. One day someone whom you have previously thought is a desirable, admirable person says that he loves you. Instead of thinking, "My, I was wrong about myself—here's someone I've always admired who says he loves me," or "Maybe I'm not so bad," or "I'm not as good as he thinks I am, but maybe I've been too hard on myself," you would think, "I was certainly wrong about him! There must be something drastically wrong with him if he loves me!"

I then began to realize that for me to live life from an internal framework that involved ebb and flow, joy and receptivity instead of fluctuations between highs and lows, pleasure and depressions, I would have to change my whole way of looking at myself and others. I became increasingly aware of how many ideas I had accepted as fact that might not be factual at all. For example, on a very simple level, I was always firmly convinced that if I went out in the rain and got my head and feet wet, I would catch a cold. Then, one or two times when that happened, I did catch a cold. What if my catching a cold was due to the belief with which I had programmed my body to react automatically rather than to any truth in that dictum?

The first step for me, then, was to take responsibility for my world. Now, this alone was not a totally new concept to me. In our work at the Family Therapy Institute, we had incorporated many of the concepts, methods, and techniques of Gestalt therapy into our growth model approach. The basic tenet of Gestalt therapy is that the individual is responsibile for his own happiness, aliveness, success, failure or loss. To blame others, fate, the world, or God is to choose to be a helpless victim who continually sets up his own demise. For example, the individual hopes that his spouse will appreciate him, but he expects that she will reject him, so he says, "You don't want to make love tonight, do you?" The theory is that we often set up situations in which we don't get what we want because we send out messages that the other person is un-giving, not interested in us, selfish, and insensitive rather than make our requests in an open manner which leaves the other person room to respond without having to convince us of his good intentions in order to be able to give to us.

For me, the new part of taking responsibility for my world had to do with the idea that if I was suffering in order to learn to live without suffering, then I wasn't doing it because there was something wrong with me or with the way I was operating. I was suffering because what I was doing was the best way I knew at that point in time to learn something that was vital to my growth that I would not have learned any other way. Now, that didn't have to mean that the process I was using wasn't painful, or restrictive, or even destructive. What it did mean was that that wasn't why I kept doing it. I kept doing it *in spite* of its limiting, destructive, or painful aspects because it was the only way I could teach myself what I needed to know. Therefore, I began to take responsibility for what was happening to me without trying to change anything, make a judgment about myself, or obsessing about why I was doing what I was doing. Think about your own life in this context for a moment. What a tremendous relief it is even to consider that, while there are things about my life I don't like and want to change, they are there because they are teaching me what I need to know in order to get what I want. They are not there because I am sick, bad, stupid, or crazy.

The next step for me, then, was to take the Gestalt principle of taking responsibility from the behavior and communication level to the energy level. Say, for example, that I have a victim process available to me. If an event occurs in my life which I find extremely painful, upsetting, or traumatic, I go into an emotional state in which I feel helpless, victimized, buffeted by fate. I react by contemplating suicide, conjuring up fantasies accompanied by terrible anxieties about what is going to happen to me, and drawing conclusions that all of this is due to how basically bad, unlucky, sinful or unappreciated I am. Or, I react by becoming vengeful. All my rules for behavior go, and I feel justified in hurting others any way I can because I am hurting so much.

Now, consider this idea. That victim process may be out of my awareness most of the time. It may come out in the open only once a year or once every two years. However, if it is available to me at all—if any event can conjure up that reaction—then, on an energy level in some layer of my consciousness, it is with me all the time. If that is so then I am emitting victim vibrations from my consciousness all of the time, even though it is not evident in my manifest behavior. Therefore, if any sadistic vibrations come into my atmosphere, it is possible that I could pull them to me like a magnet.

So, I could have an auto accident, be robbed, or be victimized in some way that seemed to be a total accident and have no connection to me whatever. There may be no apparent connection in terms of my behavior. I may be a careful driver, burglar-proof my house with the best equipment, and do all the right things to protect myself. However, on an energy level my victim emanations are attracting like energy to me. If I consider that these things are happening to me in order to teach me something valuable that I would not learn any other way, then I might be able to get in touch with my victim processes. The events that occur to me, while painful and even destructive, could also be experienced as valuable clues in teaching me how certain processes I utilize prevent me from getting what I think I want. Now, the victim process is not intrinsically bad. The use of that process, at any given point in time, may be the only way I know to slow myself down. It may keep me from reaching a degree of success, expansiveness, or depth that I am not yet ready to handle. If I become aware of the connection between external events and victim emanations on my part, I can begin to experience on a feeling level what those processes are doing for me and what they are costing me. That experience will enable me to move to the next level of my growth at a rate of progress which I can handle.

For example, I have considered that on a deep level of my consciousness I may have known I was marrying a man who was going to die and leave me, even though I had no cognitive awareness of such a possibility. When I ask myself why I let myself walk into that and why I hung onto my victim processes even after that event, I experience two answers. I reached a depth with my husband on an energy-consciousness level in which I felt one with him without losing my own identity and sense of self. The intensity of that experience was heady stuff—exciting and totally absorbing. If our relationship had continued to expand in that depth and intensity, I would have attached my ability to have such an experience to him and to that relationship instead of to me. What I have experienced since then has taught me that I create the form into which someone comes along who fits me on the level I am capable of experiencing. My ability to be alive, intense, and to relate deeply is connected to me and not dependent on a particular person or place or anything else external to me. My ability to know that makes it possible for me to go to even deeper levels of experience because I do not have to use energy to hang on to someone or something external to me—I can let go totally into the relationship or experience without fear.

I hung onto the victim framework after Merrill's death in order to learn that I was really in control of my world. In the process of recognizing my victim emanations, I learned how to let go of them and shift my energy into a positive expression. Each step of the way I saw the cause and effect, developing a full awareness of how the thoughts, fantasies and conclusions to which I attached imagery and feelings came into being. Thus my unconscious processes became conscious, and I had the beginning base for building a positive internal structure (sense of myself) based on my own natural rhythm (ebb and flow of assertion, feeling, behavior) and a burgeoning knowledge regarding how to go about creating my own world as I wanted it. I do not think that, even knowing what I know now, I would have deliberately chosen to go through the pain of that experience with my husband. But, I do believe that, on some level of my consciousness, I did decide to allow myself that experience in order to learn what I know now. I feel it would have taken me twenty years to discover what I learned in five with the route I traveled.

For the first five months of my sabbatical, when all this was going on, I kept very much to myself. I spent my time writing, studying, meditating. That sounds dull on the surface, but the experience was far from that. It had a timeless quality with the feeling that I was traveling very far but not in ways that could be measured in finite terms. In June I began to reach out and talk to some friends about what I was doing and to exchange ideas. I decided that I wanted to form a group of ten people who would meet together for six two-hour sessions. I wanted to share my ideas, get their responses and see what evolved. Originally, I planned to offer this as a course in the brochure which we sent out from the Insitutue semi-annually and take the first ten people who applied. Then, a friend of mine suggested that since the purpose of the group was to explore intuitive, energy processes, why didn't I use that method to evolve it? She suggested I write down the first ten names that occurred to me and trust that they were the appropriate people for that experience. The idea intrigued me, so I did it immediately. Twelve names occurred to me and then my mind went blank. I thought of many others later, but I decided to trust the process, write to those people and see what happened. Two of them were in Europe, but the other ten agreed to come. During our six sessions together, we had no set agenda but experimented with using in our lives the ideas all of us had evolved about intuition, energy flow, and the conscious use of energy through imagery and feeling. In addition, we experimented with a variety of techniques for the purpose of expanding consciousness like group meditation, use of the *I Ching*, * Ouija board, ESP, and Tarot cards. The input of their ideas and energy assisted me in pulling together and integrating the ideas and experiences I had had to that point. Following that experience, I felt ready to offer a seminar on a more structured basis to a wider group and began to teach that course in January. I have been amazed at how many other people are exploring the same territory—how responsive and ready so many are to take whatever risks are necessary in order to experience their aliveness to the fullest. I have subsequently taught that course many times. The teaching has stimulated me into increasingly expanded levels of thought, awareness, and sensitivity. Having to describe my experience and ideas to others has forced me to conceptualize and integrate my perceptions as I go along. I am now at the point where I feel tremendous internal pressure to put it all down on paper. I hope my excitement comes through to you as you read—it is certainly here inside of me as I am writing.

---

* Wilhelm / Baynes, *The I Ching or Book of Changes*. Princeton University Press.

5
Utilization of Energy
Toxicity

AS A BRIDGE BETWEEN THE OLD, pathologically based way of looking at behavior and a new framework based on the concepts I described earlier, I began to look at certain basic behavioral processes in terms of their use of energy, rather than seeing them as right or wrong. For example, sometimes we experience other people as toxic or poisonous to us. Have you ever spent time with someone and found the experience left you drained and depressed even though you felt fine to begin with and nothing particular happened during the visit to upset or annoy you? Or, have you known people who always leave you with the feeling that somehow you have failed, haven't done enough or have disappointed them even though nothing is said to that effect? In the therapy professions, we have often used the word toxic to describe the person or group with this "vacuum-cleaner" effect that seems to suck all the energy out of you without appearing to do so. However, that term implies that the individual is made up of bad protoplasm, possessed by some evil force, or intentionally manipulative and hurtful to others.

When I look at that vacuum-cleaner process in terms of how energy is utilized, I see a very different picture.

BODY

In this diagram, the circle represents the human organism and the lines inside represent the flow of energy internally. Now, I am not referring here to the energy body described in Kirlian photography.* That is a second body in the form of an electrical or energy field that supposedly surrounds the physical body. Now, suppose an individual is denying or repressing what he is really feeling. Have you ever been with someone whom you knew was annoyed or upset, but whose manifest communication and behavior expressed that everything was fine? Or, have you ever been in a group of people who were all furious at each other but were acting nice and polite? The atmosphere gets very heavy—you can feel the invisible pall over the room. Now, with some people, that way of operating is pervasive to their character structures. By that, I mean they are functioning that way all of the time. They have learned via early life experiences in their original families that the spontaneous expression of feeling is dangerous. They might push their parents away and find themselves feeling isolated, or they might get attacked in terms of judgments or physical abuse. Therefore, they learned to hold in what they really felt and to get what they wanted as well as protect themselves by being good, right, and obeying all the rules, even if they didn't make sense. Now, the ability to repress or deny one's own feelings is not a bad thing in and of itself. That may be the most intelligent way for a child to survive in his particular family. The energy cost in repressing his feelings may be less than the cost of isolation which would mean raising himself without any emotional assistance or utilizing enormous amounts of energy getting himself into trouble trying to change the situation. However, as he matures, the process may become increasingly costly and unnecessary, but he clings to it because it is out of his awareness that he has a choice. He operates the only way he knows. What is important is that he become aware of what he is doing, with appreciation that the process has served him well but may no longer fit where he is in his growth. Then, without the pressure of judgment forcing him any one direction, he can assess what the process costs him and what it is doing for him at any given point in time to see if he wants to let go of it.

Now, when an individual represses or denies his feelings, his internal energy is pulled inward like a vortex. It takes tremendous energy to repress one's own feeling. If the repression is pervasive—the individual is repressing most or all of his real feelings—the vortex ac-

---

* Sheila Ostrander and Lynn Schroeder, *Psychic Discoveries Behind the Iron Curtain.* Bantam Books.

tion is so strong that not only is all of his energy drawn into the process, but all of the energy with which he comes in contact is also sucked into the insatiable maw. These people often have a facial expression that reminds you of someone who has just tasted a lemon. They frequently have a dead color and seem either like automatons or invalids in their behavior. If they are trying to function with responsibilities to family and pressure jobs, they are frequently on a suicidal trail. They may not *want* to die at all. However, the energy it takes to repress feelings plus additional energy they must conjure up to cope with great external pressure is an overwhelming burden to the system, and they frequently develop severe physical symptomotology early in life—twenties, thirties, and forties.

The toxic quality of these people does not develop, then, out of any basic deformity or lack; it is a result of the sucking, vortex action of the repressive processs which pulls surrounding energy into it. Very often, in order to continue this process, the individual has not only to repress his feelings, but even keep them out of his conscious awareness so that he can operate entirely out of his head and not be confused by his intuitive level of consciousness which he does not trust and experiences as crazy. Such denial requires even greater amounts of energy to enforce, and the effort will occasionally overload the system, producing a breakdown physically or emotionally. The individual can become aware of this process via the responses he receives from others who let him know that they feel drained around him or by his own recognition of the strain on his organism. However, both he and others need to appreciate that it may not fit him to give up this process. It may be hurtful in some ways, but it has, perhaps, also enabled him to get where he is. If he gives up this process and begins to expand his intuitive, feeling levels, he may gain a great deal, but he may also lose. His marriage, his job, his whole lifestyle may not fit him if he moves into another way of functioning. In the past, I don't think I have fully appreciated this reality as a therapist. I have given the implicit message that there is a right way to be without respecting that the way in which the individual is already functioning may be the right way for him to be at this point in time in terms of the development of his entity. It sometimes doesn't fit to cure a person of a supposed illness when the illness may be serving some important function in his overall growth. As therapists, friends, family, and lovers, we are all often stymied by others' apparent lack of appreciation for our efforts to help them. I think it is important to understand that each person is responsible for his own evolutionary journey. We can offer our help, but if it is not accepted, the refusal does not have to mean that our help isn't valuable or that the other person is being stubborn or self-defeating. It may be that he hasn't finished learning what he needs to learn by the process in which he is involved.

In the overall development of his consciousness, the individual who appears as a rigid, judgmental automaton may be using this rigid external structure of right and wrong to give him something to hold onto while he is building some successful experiences. He has a touchstone while he is learning about himself enough to enable him to gradually let go as he begins to build his structure internally. The individual who appears helpless and ineffective may be using this means of forcing himself to develop his sensitive, intuitive self. If he expressed his power, he might get so caught up in the whirlwind of expansiveness that he would lose sight of the other, more subtle aspects of his consciousness. So, in terms of his evolutionary route, he has chosen a way of being that puts people off and pushes him deeper inside of himself. The "Southern Belle" or "Iron Butterfly" are well-known literary cliches. I have found that helpless-appearing people are often really very powerful on an energy level but are using tremendous strength to hold back their power. I think that on some level of consciousness that repression is deliberate, as their power would take them further and further out into the world, and they would be out of balance with their intuitive, sensitive processes.

I seem to be most helpful to others, as well as myself, when I convey the message that the individual does have a choice and that the choice is based on what is most appropriate to his growth at this time, rather than some idealized version of the right way to live, be, think, feel, function.

On the other side of the picture, if I am with someone who functions with this vortex process and I understand the process in this light, I can decide what I want to do in the relationship without having to hurt myself or make a judgment about him. I can look at the fact that I feel drained every time I am around this person, and I don't have to try to rescue him, please him, give what I don't want to give. Neither do I have to put him down as being hurtful to me, unappreciative, or basically bad. If I am not ready to let go of the relationship, I can confront him with my feelings of being drained, or I can take physical space when I feel too caught up in his process. I can also take responsibility for looking at what it is I am learning by being in a relationship with someone who operates in this way. I may choose to leave the relationship, but I do not have to judge or categorize the other person as bad in order to do it.

In my own experience, I often had difficulty letting go of a relationship unless I could diagnose what was wrong with the other person. I needed to give myself valid reasons why I should not connect with him or her so that I could leave without feeling I was wrong or that I was missing something. With this energy framework, I can let go because we are at different stages of evolution. The processes he is using for his growth are so different from the ones I am using at this point in time that I feel off balance when we are together. I can perceive my tendency to get critical or frustrated with him as an indication that I feel off balance rather than as a statement that there is something wrong with him or me. Now, I may decide to continue with the relationship on the basis that if I can learn how to stay balanced and in charge of myself with him, I can do it with anyone. That learning may be important to me in terms of my particular journey. On the other hand, I may feel I already know how to do that and it isn't worth the energy to do it with him, or it would be less costly and more effective to learn with someone whom I do not experience as so far out of balance with me.

6

Utilization of Energy Manipulation

A SECOND VERY COMMON WAY of operating has to do with a manipulative framework.

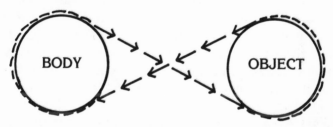

In this framework, the energy circulates around or between these two forms. The object may be animate or inanimate. If it is another person, the process is mutual. It is impossible for someone who operates with a basically manipulative framework to *maintain* a relationship with someone who does not use that process. He must either learn to let go of the manipulative process or walk away. You cannot con a non-conner, at least not for very long.

With the manipulative process, both people are manipulating for control of the other, and internal energy is mobilized to focus on external control. Again, the ability to manipulate is not of itself a negative talent. It is an extremely effective coping mechanism. A child will adopt a predominantly manipulative structure as a way of defining himself when being vulnerable and open consistently results in instrusive, judgmental, or invalidating responses. If he experiences that control of his own world is consistently taken away from him, he will fight in the best way available to him to regain that control.

I was having dinner with some friends, once, who had a three-year-old boy. While we were at the table, his father admonished him about something. When the child did not stop what he was doing, his father asked him, "Who's your boss?" Like a shot, the three-year-old pointed his thumb at his own chest and replied, *"I' m* my own boss!" His father laughed and said, "You're right—but who's your second boss?" I was impressed that that three-year-old understood so clearly that he was responsible for himself and in charge of his own choices. If the father had experienced that statement from his son as a threat rather than the child's positive appreciation of and respect for himself, he might have hit him, made fun of him, or acted hurt and withdrawn from him. If he responded consistently in these ways to his son's assertions, the child might decide that he would get what he wanted but do it in devious ways that would not be so readily challenged. He would have firmly incorporated the knowledge that being open and direct resulted in a serious loss to himself. Therefore, instead of focusing his energy on learning how to understand and express his own feelings and develop his intuitive levels of awareness, he would begin to focus his energy outside of himself, to assess the reactions of other people and gauge his behavior accordingly. The world would be perceived by him as a hostile, unpredictable place in which you could not let your guard down for a minute.

Now, the focus of energy on external control means that the organism is in a constant state of mobilization with all of its energy being focused outside like a lighthouse beacon. I believe this results in body deterioration. People who operate primarily out of a manipulative framework are subject to heart attacks and strokes at an early age because there is no opening for the flow of energy from outside. The buzz of energy between the person and the object (other person, place, or thing) he or she is attempting to control is intense and produces a tight circle—a treadmill, not going anywhere or nourishing anyone. Such a framework may produce commendable products—research, technology, money, buildings—but it sacrifices the organism to the production.

Now, according to the growth model concept, the individual would adopt a control framework because his early life experience has taught him: 1) If you aren't careful, someone will take from you what you have or will get something you want before you do. Contact with others always results in loss if you don't protect yourself. 2) It is necessary to manipulate your environment to insure nourishment and comfort. While the successful manipulator does not get nourishment in the form of energy, he does get it in terms of externals—money, sex, good food and wine, company. In fact, his ability to constantly feed himself in this way often supports him in better shape physically and for a longer period of health in his life than the person who uses repressive processes and often has life-long poor health. The manipulator's body often serves him well while it serves him but then collapses suddenly, like the one-horse shay, when he burns himself out. Deterioration takes place on an internal level as a result of being in a constant state of tension which blocks energy from flowing freely through him.

Let me explain the difference between nourishment on an energy level and nourishment by means of externals. Nourishment on an energy level takes place when the individual's defenses are down and he is unafraid, open, relaxed. In that state, he is capable of experiencing himself as one with the universe around him. He begins to experience the ebb and flow of the energy inside of himself and gradually gets in touch with his own unique internal rhythm based on the natural movement of that ebb and flow. He also develops a sense of how his own rhythm meshes with that of everything around him, and a strong sense of balance results. That sense of balance produces a serenity deep inside the individual that is nourishing and rejuvenating to the deepest recesses of body and soul. If he trusts that sense of balance and flow above all else, then his relationships, his enjoyment of pleasurable things, and the way he earns his money will intensify and expand his energy level rather than deplete it. Very simply, do you recall the difference between a sexual experience in which you were totally relaxed, willing to go with whatever emerged, and when you were "performing?"

On the other hand, when the individual operates from a state of internal tension based on having to be in control in order to survive, his savoring of whatever pleasure he engages in is blocked by that tension. His pleasure can only penetrate skin-deep, so his skin gets nourished but not his soul or consciousness. The end result is that he can expose himself to many pleasures and still feel vaguely unsatisfied.

In the past, I would have considered the manipulative processes an individual was using as detrimental to his health and blocking him from experiencing fulfilling relationships. Therefore, he obviously needed to set about changing his way of functioning. However, if I consider the same process from an energy framework (that on a deeper level of consciousness the individual is in charge and his functioning is serving some important purpose in terms of his growth, even though it is costly,) that may not be the case. For example, operating out of a control framework is forcing him to learn how to hustle. His fear and anxiety force him to keep asserting, pushing, and testing himself. He is sacrificing his intuitive levels of consciousness in the moment, but he is learning about other parts of himself. Maybe the direction he is going in terms of the evolution of his consciousness requires that he explore those parts, and this is the only, the best, or the fastest way for him to do it. Also, his adherence to a control structure, even to the extent of his own destruction, may be his way of expunging himself of it. Perhaps he has to play out the string all the way in order to let go and move on in his development. There may be a kind of purification process going on. It's also possible that the control structure provides a kind of grounding. His ability to push, organize, and manipulate circumstances, people, and events has produced certain concrete accomplishments and products. The ability to make things happen and see tangible results has given him a sense of pride in himself and his ability, not only to survive, but to create under great pressure. On a deeper level of his consciousness, which neither he nor I are in touch with, he may have made the decision that the knowledge was so vital to his overall growth it is worth any price.

To go in the direction of expanding the intuitive level of consciousness requires a strong sense of self. The individual needs a powerful inner awareness and appreciation of who he is—what are his limitations, demands, likes, dislikes, assets, liabilities, rules, values, what he wants and what he doesn't want. Without that solid awareness inside of him, the journey into expanded consciousness results in his feeling way off balance, crazy, disassociated, isolated or immobilized. The reason for that is that on that journey all constructs come into question. Our ideas about time, space, physical limitations, right and wrong—all are open to potential change. Everything external loses the illusion of solidity. If I believe that all the forms (land, food, money, oil, coal, minerals) in the world that I now see are the reality, then I have to put up with shortages, wars for space or control of resources, and societies consisting of rich and poor. That is painful, but it is comfortable in that it appears a solid, concrete reality I can touch and see. However, if I consider that all those forms are really energy, that if I could change my energy patterns I could pass through tables and chairs; if I knew the processes I could pull energy out of the atmosphere and create whatever forms I wanted, and that the supply of energy is inexhaustible; then my world would lose the dimensions that are familiar and safe to me. I may begin to feel overwhelmed or spaced-out by that prospect to the point that I want to run and hide or just become immobilized. Unless I feel so solid inside that I can tolerate total fluidity in my external environment, I will not go in that direction. In the direction of expanded consciousness there are no limitations, everything is possible; the universe is made up of "hidden treasures in secret places."* An infinitely exciting or potentially terrifying prospect, depending on my internal state. I feel we are all moving toward that experience, but each in his own, unique, inimitable fashion. I have unqualified faith in the ability of each organism, on some level of his consciousness, to choose the way that is necessary and best for his evolution. Each of us is continually modifying, expanding, polishing, exploring, defining some aspect of our consciousness or energy system all of the time, even though it may not be immediately evident to ourselves or others.

---

* Isaiah 45:3, The *Bible*.

7
Utilization of Energy Psychosis

A THIRD FRAMEWORK has to do with what we label as psychotic. In our society, when we diagnose someone as mentally ill, we figuratively and often literally put him in a box and close the lid. We communicate to him on a feeling level that he doesn't make any sense, is dangerous, or is damaged goods. Our best behavior toward him consistently communicates one or all of these messages even though it proceeds under the guise of treatment or tender, loving care. We consistently deny that anything he is experiencing is real. We assume that we are in touch with reality and he is not, as though our knowledge of reality was all there is. What if the psychotic is in touch with another reality with no bridge to tie it back to the concrete, tangible world he has known? I perceive his internal energy flow in this way:

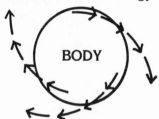

The energy flow is not blocked, but it is arhythmic. It has spaces in it, spasms, or fibrillations like a heart that is not functioning normally. I feel this energy arhythmia is due to a lack of clarity in the individual about his own identity. He experiences himself as amorphous with no solidity. Thus, data from other energy sources filters into his system, but he does not have enough grounding in his sense of himself and his own evolutionary development to determine what belongs to him and what belongs to someone else, let alone how to handle it. Because he is so off balance that he doesn't question anything, he may also be available to data that the rest of us close

46

off. For example, suppose the voices he hears are real? We know that dogs have a much more developed sense of hearing than we do and hear many sounds totally out of our current range. Suppose there were many voices in the atmosphere around us. Science says energy cannot be created or destroyed. Voices are energy. Therefore, perhaps we can assume that every word ever spoken is still available to us if we were open to that possibility and knew how to listen. If we considered that a so-called psychotic person had data available to him that we didn't, and we explored with him on that basis, perhaps we could learn a great deal. In addition, he would be getting a message from us that what he was experiencing might have great value rather than indicating he is sick or dangerous. If he got that kind of message from us, who knows how differently he would respond?

With the person who thinks he is Napoleon or Jesus Christ, who are we to say that isn't so? Suppose that in the makeup of his energy system there is some of the same energy that was part of Napoleon or Jesus and that on some level of his consciousness he has a memory of that experience. Perhaps the deja vu experiences that we consider a normal part of everyday existence are very real memories of our expanded selves in another time or place. If we considered that there might be many parts of us on an energy level which we are not aware of and that these parts might be connected to what we would experience as other lives or times, perhaps such information would come to us. As long as we reject any possibility of such data being real, we automatically close off awareness. The part of each of us that is directing our growth will not push us into any expansion for which we are not ready. The psychotic person, on the other hand, loses his sense of balance or reality. Because nothing makes sense to him anymore, then everything is possible. He loses his ability to make any sense and order out of his life experience. Therefore, he opens himself up to data which his consciousness might otherwise reject because it didn't make sense.

When the psychotic person describes his hallucinations, suppose we considered that they might be real. Perhaps he is seeing auras which we now know actually exist.* If auras are real, perhaps faces, bodies, forms of all kinds can appear and disappear, should we be

---

* Ostrander and Schroeder, *Psychic Discoveries.*

willing to lift the blinds from our eyes. Consider that the linear progression of time is an illusion that we cling to for some semblance
of solidity and continuity. Perhaps everything is really all happening
at once on an energy level, and our sense of time is based on what
we choose to be aware of in the moment. If time barriers are artificial,
then perhaps I could conjure up scenes from the "past" or "future"
by simply opening up more windows in my consciousness to let in
more data. If I thought that was possible, I might learn how to do
it. As long as I don't think it's possible, it isn't. Every concrete reality
was originally a dream or vision (telephone, airplane, electric light).
Again, I do not have to believe anything—I can escalate my growth
just by refusing to reject possibilities. The psychotic person may be
getting flooded with such data simply because his defenses are down
and he is not blocking anything. However, he is not utilizing the data
either because he does not have a solid internal structure which
enables him to assimilate, define, and integrate the data with his
already existing framework.

In my capacity as a therapist, I originally saw psychosis as a totally
negative state requiring immediate and often drastic measures which
I felt might arrest the process, but it was questionable the patient
could ever be cured. As I adopted the growth model concept, I shifted
to looking at psychosis as a temporary emotional state in which the
structure on which an individual had depended for survival and security had broken down leaving him with nothing solid on which to rely.
For example, in the *Caine Mutiny*, Captain Queeg's rigid structure
of going by the book with no variations carried him to the top of his
profession but began to deteriorate under the stress of emergencies
for which the book didn't have answers. Psychosis also resulted from
an individual's inability to build any structure at all because his early
life situation did not provide enough nurturance and stability to give
him an opportunity to find out who he was and experiment with ways
of expressing himself to determine what fit for him. So, he remained
unformed and fragmented in his sense of himself. Treatment involved providing external supports in the form of hospitalization, day care,
and/or medication to reduce his anxiety enough so that he could utilize
therapy for the purpose of beginning to understand himself and
develop his identity.

Psychosis could also develop in an individual who experienced impossible demands in his family system. The external message was, "Be a man," but when he tried to assert himself, his parents either attacked, judged, or withdrew from him. If he tried to comment on the discrepancy between what they said and what they did, they induced guilt (he didn't understand or appreciate them) or again attacked or withdrew. He consistently received such double messages, so he assumed he could not win unless he was crazy. Then, no one would hold him responsible for anything. Treatment in this instance involved working with the whole family to make the double messages explicit and to enable them to break down whatever barriers were in the way toward their communicating clearly and directly. If the family could not be involved in treatment, then the individual was helped to see consciously and understand the bind to which he was reacting. Then he could decide if he wanted to stay connected to his family at the cost of being "crazy" or if he wanted to learn how to assert for himself at the risk of alienating them.

In all of these instances, the psychosis is attributed to inadequate or distorted learning and not to a deformity or inadequacy in the individual. It is, therefore, part of a learning process and not a fixed, immutable state. Within the context of the energy framework, I believe that all of that is still true. However, even with this approach, there are people who will not give up a psychotic process. I now see that choice differently. It may be that in a psychotic state an individual may experience extreme terror, but in this state of heightened sensitivity he may also taste excitement connected to the realization that there are other worlds, other states of being that we reject in our normal reality. It may be like having a taste of space travel before any ship had ever been built to make such a trip tangible.

It is also possible that an individual would choose to adopt a psychotic state in order to experience a degree of helplessness and isolation that would enable him to develop a kind of depth and understanding unavailable to him otherwise. That particular kind of depth may be a vital part of his learning in terms of his overall journey. It may also be important for him to realize his worse fears—going crazy—so that he can exorcise himself of that shadowy demon and proceed without fear.

I believe now that there is no such thing as insanity in terms of a fixed state. Suppose there were twenty people in a locked room.

Pretend that nineteen of them were brainwashed to believe they were having fun at a party. One person could see out of a huge window at the end of the room that a tidal wave was coming their way. You are viewing the scene, but you cannot see the window or the wave. The one person is jumping up and down frantically, trying to get everyone to help him break down the door. Everyone else is laughing and talking. It looks to you as if the one man is insane. Then your view shifts, and you can see the window and the tidal wave. Now, it seems to you that the nineteen others are insane. Then you are made aware that nineteen have been brainwashed while one has not, and you realize that in that context everyone's behavior is rational. Suddenly the scene disappears; you "wake up" realizing you have had a dream, and you wonder if *you* are rational. So, as we open up to an expanded view of ourselves, all of our fixed reference points begin to shift and then disappear. Thus, in order for us to evolve without total chaos, our expansion of consciousness must coincide and balance with the development of our identity both individually and culturally. As I become more trusting of my intuitive processes and the basic wholeness and goodness of my inner self, I can let go of my external supports without fear of destruction or loss. As I trust me, I also increase my trust of you, and I can focus less energy on protecting me from you or you from me.

8
Utilization of Energy
Unblocked Energy Structure

A FOURTH FRAMEWORK I DESCRIBE as an unblocked energy structure. The individual's internal energy is flowing in synchrony with his natural rhythm so that he is not fighting himself. By that I mean he asserts but does not force himself to push beyond what fits for him. He follows through but does not hang on inappropriately. He trusts his feelings and uses them as the basis for determining his life's direction. His trust builds as he experiments with his feelings and finds out they support growth and not destruction. With that trust comes a strong sense of who he is since his feelings are what determine his uniqueness. His energy moves in an unbroken, unblocked ebb and flow. It is possible just to look at him and see exactly where he is—whether he is feeling sad, happy, warm, subdued or peaceful.

Thus the flow of energy from outside (other people, events, the atmosphere) passes into his system and is touched, absorbed, repelled or dissipated in the process. For example, a friend becomes ill, and

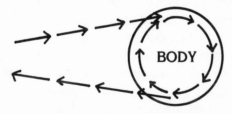

you go to visit him in the hospital. He looks drawn, and you can tell he is feeling badly. Instead of trying to cheer him up, which would be forcing yourself to go in a direction contrary to your feelings, or ignoring his pain, which would require you to utilize energy to hold your feelings down, you sit with him and let yourself feel his pain without making any demands on yourself. As you experience his feelings and your own, you may be moved to say something, you may not. You and he are communicating on an energy level. He can experience that you are really there for him because you are letting him inside of yourself—there is no greater gift. After you leave the hospital, his pain and your concern for him linger with you. You allow yourself to feel his pain, your own sadness, and your concern for him, and you find yourself weeping softly as you drive home. As the tears flow, there is a sense of relief and comfort in the awareness that you have given to yourself and your friend the gift of remaining open to life and its flow. You continue to be open to the next experience.

In another instance, you are making love with someone for whom you have deep feelings. You each stay focused on your own feelings knowing that there is no separation on an energy level, so that whatever you are feeling your partner is also feeling or is responding to in some way. As you stay with this awareness, there is no need to perform. On an energy level, the process is always mutual. If one is pleased, the other is pleased. If one is distant, the other feels it. If one is angry, the other feels it. If each feels open to his own and the other's feelings, there is a sense of merging like one cloud moving into, through, and around another, without any loss in terms of its own substance or sense of its own entity. You feel the other person's feelings as though they are your own, and yet you do not lose yourself in the process. You are so connected to your own feelings that you can always differentiate between yours and those of another, even when they are the same. You do not doubt that what you are feeling belongs to you just because the other person feels the same thing so strongly. You are not fearful of losing your joy because you allow yourself to feel the other person's pain.

You may meet someone whom you perceive as emotionally draining to you. You are able to move away in the moment without focusing energy on who is right or wrong or on making conclusions about the future. You trust your feelings without having all the answers. In the same way, you make contact with someone whose energy you experience as intense, joyous and unbounded. It does not fit with your current emotional state which is subdued and introspective. Instead of depreciating yourself for not responding to the other person's joy or having to find a reason to distance from him, you accept that you are off balance with each other at that point in time because of your polarized emotional states. You can then take distance without depreciating yourself or him.

If you are in a group in which you perceive high energy and joy, you can allow that energy into your own system. As you savor that high charge and allow it to intensify and expand your own energy, you can then focus it outward with more power than that with which it entered your system. It is as though I was a mechanic in a room full of precision tools. Nothing would happen to the automobile in front of me until I picked up one of those tools. Then the inherent power in that appliance would accomplish a task, produce a result. The same process occurs on an energy level. Energy around us can be experienced by our own internal energy systems and re-focused with expanded power like a laser beam.

I feel that the circulation of energy within the individual in an unbroken flow depends on a balance among the processes of intuition, assertion, experiential exploration, and integration. In order for the individual to grow in the direction of expanded levels of consciousness, he must rely on his intuitive processes for the direction of his life. Some part of his consciousness is in touch with the ebb and flow of the Universe around him and with how his own rhythm fits into that overall pattern. His intuitive processes are the route to a greater understanding of that flow on all levels of his energy system. As he experiments with expressing how he feels and acting on his feelings, he learns ways of doing this that are fitting to his personality and that get his messages across clearly to others. As he asserts, he sees the effect of what he says and does, he gets responses from other people about what they like and don't like, how they see him and feel toward him. He takes that data—how his assertions make him feel about himself and how they make others feel about him—puts it together with his value system and what he knows about where he has been in his development and where he wants to go. Out of that process, he decides what fits for him in terms of who he is and integrates that knowledge into an internal structure which feels increasingly clear and solid to him as the process continues. With that increasing sense of clarity and solidity, he feels more trusting of himself and more comfortable with his feelings. As that occurs, his process intensifies, and he becomes increasingly sensitive, intuitive, and assertive. He begins to experience himself like a buoy on water. The water can get extremely choppy and unpredictable, but he maintains his balance.

Such internal balance gives impetus to movement toward external balance in the areas of the:

A) Physical body: He finds himself moving without effort in the direction of experimenting with nutrition and exercise to determine what is fitting for him. In the process, he learns that his body is unique in the sense that no one else's rules fit totally, and he has to trust his feelings and his body responses to determine his own rules. He learns how to discipline himself based on filling up his system and his time with what is beneficial and joyful to him rather than focusing his energy on denying himself things that are not good for him. He finds that if his energy is focused on what works, the negative will dissipate on its own. He finds that his sensitivity and sensuality are heightened—colors are brighter, food tastes better, relationships are more intense. He begins to experience a rhythm and a flow between himself and what he does, without a compulsion to grab or hang on for fear he will miss something. He begins to trust that his own inner rhythm will put him in touch with what is good for him at any point in time because he is synchronized with the innate rhythm of the Universe.

B) Cognitive apparatus: He begins to shift his value system from a right-wrong framework based on fear of punishment, loss of freedom, or guilt. Instead, he determines his values on the basis of energy laws which have to do with cause and effect. For example, as he deepens his experience of himself on an intuitive level, his sense of separateness from others becomes increasingly illusory. He perceives himself on a consciousness level as one with all around him. From that awareness, it is clear that he cannot rip off energy from someone else without ripping it off from himself. If they are one, there is no way to do that. Thus, if he wants to steal, he must decide if he can afford to lose fifty or one hundred dollars worth of energy at that point in time, rather than worry about whether he is justified in the theft or whether he will get caught. On an energy level, there is no getting away with anything. Our current "energy shortage" is loud evidence of this. There is simple cause and effect. If we take without putting back, we will eventually lose. Not because we are being punished, but because we are all one and the same even though different. By the same process, if we put energy into the system, we will be buoyed and replenished. Not because we are virtuous, but because we are utilizing an immutable, impersonal law.

C) **Emotional centeredness:** As the individual grows in his awareness of his intuitive processes and his sense of his own rhythm in synchrony with the rhythm of the Universe, he attaches his emotional survival, his comfort, and his sense of power to that phenomena rather than to someone or something outside of himself. He develops total trust in his ability on an energy level to create and control his own world according to energy laws, and basic trust in his own wholeness and goodness.

Thus, each of these aspects of the personality (sense of own and universal rhythm, physical well-being, cognitive apparatus, emotional centeredness) all come together like musical chords, the sum of whose parts bursts forth in the brilliant sound of perfect harmony. When the organism has optimum balance, it explodes into a new dimension.

9
Energy Laws

I BELIEVE THERE ARE ENERGY LAWS that operate in the Universe with the same inexorable cause and effect mechanisms that operate in physical laws such as gravity. These are the primary energy laws which I perceive:

A. Thoughts are energy and have power. We create forms according to the thoughts and images to which we vibrate. The process is magnetic—drawing us to people, places, and things which fit those forms. The vibration phenomena involves imagining a picture in my mind's eye and then letting myself experience my feelings about that picture as though it was a concrete reality. I can do this with either negative or positive pictures. If I picture some disaster befalling me, feel great anxiety about my impending disaster, and keep focusing consistently on that image with its negative emotional accompaniment; I will eventually bring disaster about. It may not take the exact form I pictured, but some disaster will occur. The ingredients are the picture, the accompanying feeling or energy vibration, and the consistent focus. Fleeting disaster images do not have the same impact unless there are many of them, and we experience them with some regularity. That is a clue that, on some level of consciousness, we are harboring a Greek tragedy script. This process is learned, which is why some families actually appear to operate as though they were playing out a Greek tragedy—with seemingly accidental disasters befalling them one after another.

By the same token, we can create a positive image of what we want, vibrate to that image (hold on to it and let ourselves enjoy it,) and set in motion the processes that make it a concrete reality. Have you ever dreamed of a house you wanted and spent time and energy planning every detail, including the furnishings? Then, at some point in your life, that house appeared concretely, so similar in form to your dream that it seemed like a miracle? Most of us have had this experience on a smaller scale with a piece of clothing, furniture, automobile. But you say, "I have had many dreams that didn't come to pass." Take a look at how many times you dream a dream, but your vibrations say, "It isn't possible, it won't happen, don't get your hopes up because you'll only be disappointed."

How often have you read "success" stories in which the hero claimed that no matter what happened, he never gave up his dream. He lost several investments before he made his first million; she struggled against insurmountable odds, but managed to walk or skate or swim again. Without exception, the achiever is someone who had a dream from which he never deviated for a moment.

B. No one can use the energy process to intrude on another's journey. We can determine what we want, but we cannot program the timing, the people involved, or the way in which our wishes will be carried out. We have to trust that the law operates so that everything and everyone fit, and there is much that we cannot see or do not know on our cognitive level. Our expanded levels of consciousness have this information, but we may not be totally in touch with those other levels and are, therefore, limited in the knowledge available to us in the moment. For example, I may want a particular man to love me. If I attempt to control him and force him to me with this energy process, I may set in motion a self-defeating phenomena. On one hand, I am sending out positive vibrations that I want him. On the other, I am sending out vibrations on an enegy level that are controlling and domineering, because my behavior implies I want him whether it fits for him or not. He is picking up both vibrations on an energy level and may avoid me without actually knowing why, even though he may find me attractive. He doesn't want to be controlled.

On the other hand, he may be harboring victim processes on some level of his consciousness which would allow him to be drawn into a relationship, even though it doesn't really fit him in terms of his basic rhythm. Thus, he and I could get together and have a miserable marriage, in terms of being happy and fulfilled. However, on an evolutionary basis, such a detour may be necessary for purposes of growth. We may utilize the relationship to learn how to let go of our control and victim processes which are getting in the way of our getting what we really want.

If I want to utilize the law without sabotaging myself, I would imagine the kind of man I want and how I would like us to feel toward each other, then trust my intuitive levels of consciousness to draw into my orbit the actual person who fits that form most satisfactorily for him and for me, at the time most appropriate for both of us. As you can see, this would take a high level of trust, and I would get in touch with all the negativity in my system (doubts and fears) as I experimented with the process. Thus, I would get a picture of all the ways in which I had previously defeated myself so that I could begin to expunge myself of that negativity. Personally, I did not realize how much doubt, fear, and negation I was harboring in my system until I began to take conscious charge of my creative process.

I want to make it clear that the process I describe, of vibrating to what is positive rather than to the negative, does not mean I deny those experiences I perceive as negative and pretend they aren't happening. I'm sure you have heard or read of situations in which people refused medical assistance with the faith they were not really ill and then died. Or, someone smiles or keeps a stiff upper lip, saying "It's God's will; therefore, I shouldn't be upset or sad." On the contrary, I feel it is very important to face directly whatever is happening to you and allow yourself to feel sad, angry, frustrated, or whatever other reaction the situation triggers. The ability to savor or wallow in a feeling, until we experience it in every fiber of our being, promotes growth. However, very often, the next step we take is a negative one. We make assumptions that what has happened is due to fate, bad luck, punishment, or a basic, inherent inability on our part to do any better. We then draw conclusions that we will continue to be second-class citizens, patients, losers, or mediocre all our lives, and we vibrate to those conclusions as though they were factual and irreversible.

Instead, we might allow ourselves to perceive whatever ever occurs in the present, experience totally whatever it is we feel in response to that perception, but hold to our image of the way we want things to be and vibrate to that image as our reality. Everything else is only part of the process of getting there. If we hold consistently to that reality, we utilize an energy law and bring about our desire as surely as night follows day. It is as though I pulled molecules ou of the air and created a chair. Then I operate as though the chair, rather than the molecules, is the reality. On that basis, there is only room for one of us to sit down, and already we have a shortage. However, if I keep my focus on the molecules as the reality, then the supply is unlimited, and I can create all the chairs I want in any number or quantity. We operate as though the concrete forms we observe are the reality, and we consistently fight over them. Consider that the energy of which those forms consist is the reality, and, because it is constantly evolving and expanding—never static, it is inexhaustible.

C. Unconditional love. In my work as a therapist, the human being's quest for unconditional love is a persevering one, no matter how often we hear or read that such love is a myth. At this point in my life, I believe that such love is a reality. The myth is that we assume it must be obtained from our parents or some individual other than ourselves. So the unending search goes on for the brass ring—the person who will love us for ourselves no matter what we do or say.

I believe there is a law of unconditional love that relates to our expanded levels of consciousness. Let's assume there is a center of consciousness inside each of us that does know all the answers and is unerring in its direction of the evolution of ourselves. Then, much of our difficulty stems from lack of contact between that expanded level of consciousness and the concrete, cognitive level of ourselves. Cognitively, we tend to judge ourselves in terms of external success. If we get a certain job, produce concrete results, make money, win plaudits, and receive love, we feel happy with ourselves. If circumstances and relationships do not produce our desired results, we are critical of ourselves, judgmental about our worth, and depreciating in our attitudes toward ourselves. We add insult to injury by trying to force ourselves in a direction we don't want to go because that route might be more productive, successful, right or good. We may try to change something we're doing by a sheer act of will, and, if we fail to change, we dump additional ashes on our heads.

The kinds of struggles we get into with people who are close to us are very often external representations of the wars going on inside each of us. For example, I may frequently find myself in a power struggle with my husband over who is right or wrong in an issue. No matter what we start to discuss, we end up with each of us presenting evidence about his or her position to convince the other, rationalize or justify our behavior, or explain ourselves to each other. We feel frustrated, unresolved, and dissatisfied. If I begin to look at my internal dialogue with myself, I begin to realize that I have the same process going on even when no one else is around. I find myself obsessing about whether or not I did the right thing, rationalizing and explaining my behavior to myself, condemning myself for being wrong, bad, inadequate. My relationships are external reflections, mirrors of the relationship I have with myself.

I feel that as long as an individual maintains this basic distrust of himself, he will often feel frustrated and hopeless, and he will have a rocky road in his life's journey. I think that his more expanded level of consciousness will be in charge and will continue to push him toward growth, but it has to fight his rational, cognitive level to do that. So, often the only way to get through to him is to clobber him. For example, the men and women who have heart attacks and then live a long time without another attack are the ones who drastically change their lifestyles. They revise their diets, they exercise, they reduce stress in their lives—they move toward a more balanced, joyous way of living instead of driving themselves frantically. The ones who revert to their former pre-attack lifestyles continue to have attacks until they change or die. The same thing occurs on an energy level. Something inside of us pushes us toward greater aliveness, very often by confronting us dramatically with how we are killing ourselves. My experience has been that most people who become seriously ill have previously had more subtle warnings for years which they did not heed.

Warnings come in the form of illness, accidents, coincidences, dissatisfaction. If we are in harmony with our own rhythm and the rhythm of the world around us, we feel joy, aliveness, and have perfect health. Any variation in these states indicates we are off the track in our evolutionary journey. However, there are even more subtle clues. Usually, when we run across a barrier or minor irritant in our path, we get frustrated, try to force our way through. If that fails, we give up and feel worthless. If, instead, we considered that that barrier or irritant was a clue that in some way we were out of synchrony with our own rhythm or the energy around us, then we could experience that interruption as valuable data to utilize for deepening our awareness of our rhythm. We often function on the basis that a particular outcome is desirable or worthwhile only if it is difficult to come by. We feel virtuous when we have had to manipulate, maneuver, put ourselves through a wringer in some way to accomplish something. It is as though "I have paid my dues—now I can enjoy myself!" I think that the opposite is true. That which is most beneficial to us, most productive of aliveness and growth, is accomplished smoothly and easily. When an outcome evolves with ease and fluidity, the satisfaction we receive is deeper, truer and lasting.

Accomplishment that evolves out of a sense of aliveness has a timeless, flowing quality to it. The only way we realize how much we have done is to look back on where we were and compare it to where we are in the moment. There is no sense of time going by, no ennui, no sense of force or push. It is not a passive, drifting state. We are asserting, but as if through thick cream or plush velvet, not quicksand or barbed wire. We make contact with difficulties as we assert, but they dissolve in front of us. If they do not, we look at them as indications we are off our pathway; we stay with our uncertainties until a new direction emerges from our intuitive levels, and we evolve in that direction.

In this context, we are exercising a continual appreciation of ourselves. This is my understanding of the meaning of unconditional love. I appreciate that some part of me, which may be out of my conscious awareness, is directing me. I appreciate that it is doing the best it can with the knowledge and awareness I have available to me in the moment. Therefore, the processes I am utilizing for learning may be somewhat limiting, unpleasant, or even destructive, but they are all I have, at this point in time, to learn what I need to know. If I give myself that kind of appreciation, I consider everything that happens to me in the light of what the more expanded aspect of my consciousness is trying to teach me. When I do that, the war is over, and I take conscious charge of my growth process. I stop fighting myself. With that shift, I automatically open up the channel between the intuitive, expanded levels of my consciousness and my cognitive level. As long as I criticize, judge, and try to force myself in any direction or deny what I am feeling, I keep that channel closed. The intuitive, alive part of me still directs me, but it is an uphill battle. When I let go and begin to appreciate that I am responsible for everything that happens to me because it is a vital learning experience in terms of my growth, that is unconditional love! When I give myself that kind of love and appreciation, I open myself up to the subtleties and nuances of my internal teacher, available to me through my intuitive processes. Then I begin to sense the rhythm and pulsation of life and to taste what real excitement is.

D. The only reason for suffering is to learn how to live without suffering. We are defeated by the assumption, passed down through generations, that despair, illness, and anguish are a natural part of human development and must be accepted as such. We hear that we cannot appreciate joy unless we have suffered so we have some basis for comparison. We tell our children not to glory in themselves because they will become selfish or conceited. Nothing is worthwhile unless it is achieved through pain. We all want to love, to be loved, and to be creative in our lives. We try to achieve those states by making sure we don't think too highly of ourselves, channeling our energies into rigid structures that may or may not fit us, and criticizing ourselves harshly for any deviation from the hard-working, self-effacing, mass-producing image we have constructed for ourselves. It seems ludicrous to expect that we would achieve love and creativity via those channels. Yet, perhaps we have had to try in order to know that that is not the route. In our experience, we prove the fallacy of that route over and over. On the other hand, perhaps we have needed our rigid structures to lean on until we felt strong enough to risk trusting ourselves.

E. We can create our own world by the thoughts, images, and fantasies to which we vibrate. We are not victims. There are two men who are currently exhibiting awesome feats to the world. They are Jack Schwartz and Swami Rama. Both of them have been examined extensively by various medical and research groups. Jack Schwartz can push a knitting needle through his arm and control whether or not the arm bleeds during the process, then remove the needle with no injury, infection or bleeding. Swami Rama can produce and dissolve body tumors at will. Both men indicate the mind is capable of being in touch with every aspect of the body down to the most minute cell and that the mind recreates the body constantly. They are in conscious charge of that process and indicate that all of us could be.

At this point in our development, we live with the belief that we have a conscious and an unconscious mind. The conscious mind deals with the tangible and concrete—logic, reason, will, and feelings connected to persons, places, things we can touch or see or hear. The unconscious houses the unknown—intuition, hunches, precognition, telepathy, visions, dreams, fantasies, sensations, images, esp. I think that the separation between these two minds is artificial—there only because we have assumed it should be. The Yogis have always maintained that the body is a creation of the mind.* I believe that the experiments with Jack Schwartz and Swami Rama have made that assertion an evident fact. The potential power we have is awesome if the unconscious mind is brought into conscious awareness. The mind then becomes one with the body and with the energy around us.

However, the route to conscious awareness of the unconscious is not through the intellect or logic. Einstein once said that a mystic impulse had told him his formula for the theory of relativity was true and there must be proof of it. Others could work it out, prove it step by step, but he *knew*. Logic alone, carried to the infinite, means nothing, goes nowhere. Remember the story of the man who drowned in water that *averaged* two inches in depth? Or, how many times have you tried to buy a car or some other object and logically weighed all the pros and cons of price, durability, and performance; then you chose what you wanted on the basis of color, looks, or because you just had to have it? I do not intend to demean logic. The ability to be logical and rational is a commendable talent. I am saying that it is not sufficient unto itself. What does it mean if you do all the right things, make all the right moves so that you are respected, wealthy, and famous, if you do not feel alive? On a recent segment of the "Kung Fu" television show, I heard a character say a line to the effect that, "If you go through life alone, you lose love. If you go through life with someone whom you do not love, you lose your soul." How many people who have done all the right things live lives of quiet desperation?

The route to making the unconscious conscious is through the intuition. Most of us have developed our rational, logical minds way out of proportion to the rest of us because our education focuses on that aspect of our consciousness. That development and that learn-

* Yogananda, *The Autobiography of a Yogi.* Self-Realization Fellowship.

ing is valuable, but we must set it aside temporarily in order to develop the other aspects of our consciousness because logic gets in the way. To expand consciousness, the intuitive, feeling aspects must be in the lead. We must be willing to take the risk to assert our feelings and follow our intuitive director. That doesn't mean we have to discard all our logic and jump impulsively into some kind of chaotic acting-out. Some people may do it that way, but there is no *one* way. It doesn't make any difference how often we act on a feeling as long as we feel we *are* doing it and are moving and growing in the direction of increasing trust in our feelings. Each person has his own rhythm and pace for change and growth, and that rhythm is best for him. As we give our feelings more and more power to direct us, the intellect becomes the follower. It evaluates what happens when we assert our feelings, determines what is fitting to our particular personalities, and integrates that experience into an internal structure which is the individual's sense of self. As we train the mind to look for the growth aspect in all that we do, the channel between the cognitive apparatus and the intuitive self opens until they become one. At that point, we will react, often instantaneously, with a feeling and an understanding of what the feeling means at the same time. For example, some months ago I went downtown to do some shopping. By mistake, I pulled into the wrong line to enter a parking garage. A man suddenly appeared at my window, his face livid, and shouted at me for being in the wrong place and adding the last straw to his already frustrating day. He said his piece and huffed away without giving me a chance to respond. I pulled out of the line, angry, hurt, feeling unjustly attacked and misunderstood, and surprised myself by abruptly bursting into tears. Not only did I burst into tears, but I found myself sobbing with gasps that seemed to come from the feet up. I allowed myself to just flow with the feeling without trying to stop it, analyze it, or understand it. However, I realized that, without any conscious directing, a part of me was automatically saying, "Now why did you set *this* up?" The question was occupying my mind in perfect comfort, along with the intense feeling. Neither was interfering with the other. They were operating separately and yet together. The answer came immediately. I had done a number of things that week that I didn't really want to do. I had done them for a variety of reasons—a friend needed me, my business required it, it would make something easier in the future, et cetera. However, the price I had paid for going against myself was the build-up of some negativity in my system—resentment on my part, and bad vibrations from some of the situations in which I had been involved. I realized I had allowed this current situation to happen in order to trigger the tears, put me in touch with my process, and cleanse my system of the negativity I had built up or absorbed. In the future I might make the same choices, but I would know what it was costing me and perhaps find some safety valves along the way to prevent the negative build-up. All of this awareness happened instantaneously along with the tears. When the feeling had washed over and through me, I felt relieved and cleansed, even to the extent that I could picture the man and send him the wish that he could be relieved of whatever burden he was carrying.

F. Each of us wields power constantly. The vibrations we choose to support enhance or distort our own evolutionary trip and enhance or distort the evolutionary trip of everyone who comes into our atmosphere. Now, it is not possible for me to change someone else's journey or pathway. However, I can make it easier or more difficult for him. For example, when you are around someone whom you feel is alive and in charge of himself, you feel free to be whoever you are and to stay with your own feelings in the moment. If the other person is functioning in such a way that he is pulling energy from those around him, you have difficulty staying with your own growth. You may utilize your energy to take care of him, or to feel resentful and obsess about his intrusion on you, or to figure out ways to take care of yourself in the presence of his depletion of energy. Therefore, the greatest gift I can give another person is to take responsibility for my aliveness. With that awareness, it becomes ludicrous to think that I am helping someone by sacrificing myself. When I sacrifice myself, I feel resentful, depressed, victimized, hopeless or depressed. I may be doing something that is helping the other person physically, but I am sapping his life's energy by the way in which I am handling my own energy. Real communication takes place on the energy level. Anything we do or say that does not coincide with what we are experiencing on that level is a farce.

I have found that many people shy away from seeing themselves as powerful. I feel that if we accept that we have power over our lives and are not victims of fate, then we realize that there is no way out. Perhaps death is not even a way out. As in Shakespeare's soliloquy for Hamlet—who knows in that sleep of death what dreams may come? People talk about being afraid of death, but I feel we are more afraid of life than death. The idea of death is often comforting—it is a release, a way out. When I talk to clients now who are contemplating suicide, I suggest to such a person that perhaps he has two choices he hasn't considered. He can accept that he set up the circumstances that are so painful to him in order to learn something vital and imperative to his particular journey. Perhaps he bit off more than he can chew and set up too difficult a task for himself. If so, he may decide to end this life. However, it may also be possible that if he doesn't work out his task here and now, he may have to do it somewhere else at another time and place. If he could stick with it now and learn whatever he has to learn by this experience, he might speed up his overall journey so that he can leave suffering behind him and move into expansiveness and joy. If he leaves, the journey may be easier, but also slower and longer. So, the choice may not be whether or not he wants to face whatever issues he is facing; the choice may be between a journey that is difficult, but fast, and one that is less arduous, but slow. I don't really care if someone believes that in the way that I do. What I want to do is raise doubt that death is a way out. I think that concept is in question.

In many philosophical and religious treatises there are stories about prophets or religious leaders who did not die in the sense that they became ill or were killed. They made a decision to leave the body and left, without having to hurt or destroy the body in any way to make passage possible. I have always thought those stories were parables, or perhaps miracles belonging to another time that I didn't understand. However, now I wonder if death, on an energy level, is simply just a passage over which we could also have conscious charge if we opened up our minds to that possibility. The opening is the precursor to the knowledge that makes such phenomena possible. Nothing is learned unless the mind opens a passageway. The opening may begin with doubt of the old dicta; then questions about new, previously unacceptable possibilities; then trust in the intuitive level to guide toward making the unknowable knowable.

At any rate, to accept that one has power to create one's world means that when we give up, let go, or run and hide, we are only delaying the journey. That is all right; we may have a good reason for delay. However, we cannot avoid the reality that the only way to the promised land is through ourselves. No one is going to come along and make everything all right. No miracle is going to occur from the outside to change our experience. The route to joy is through the evolution of our consciousness. We can fight and scream and kick our heels, or we can give up in despair. But we must inevitably come back to the inexorable truth that each of us is in charge of his own salvation.

G. Oneness. On an energy level we are one, expressing the same energy or consciousness through our unique channels. There is a verse in the Bible which says, "There is a variety of gifts but always the same spirit ... "* In his latest book,* Paul Williams says, in effect; if you could look into space and see without any limitations, what would you see? The back of your head, of course. The flow of energy is circular, moving in ripples inevitably back to the source. We live with the illusion of separateness because we accept the concrete as our only reality. Therefore, because you and I have different bodies, we are separate. Because we are thousands miles apart, we are separate. Because we live in different houses, we are separate. On an energy level there is no time or space or concrete dimension. My consciousness is part of a universal ebb and flow so that if someone throws in a rock, eventually I will feel its tremor and so will he.

On that level, stealing or killing becomes ludicrous. It does not even matter what we believe or care about right or wrong. The implacable law is that if I rip off energy from you in any form—money, property, life, aliveness—the vibrations will eventually return and rip off energy from me. It is impossible for it to be otherwise, because we are part of the same consciousness. Therefore, my choice always is—do I want to steal energy now and take the consequences of energy loss to myself in the future? By the same token, if I expand my energy by taking responsibility for my aliveness, that energy adds to the power of the ripples in the stream so that, when the stream of consciousness ebbs and flows, its power builds and enriches us all. When my freely flowing energy meets your freely flowing energy there is

---

* 1 Corinthians 12:4.
* Paul Williams, *Das Energi.* Electra Books, 1973.

an automatic intensification that expands the energy of us both without taking anything from either.

H. Energy is not static. Therefore, it is unlimited. Energy is capable of unlimited expansion and intensification. If we focus on energy as our reality, there are no shortages. We do not have to have rich and poor, have and have-nots. Everyone can have everything he wants to enhance his aliveness as long as it does not inhibit his own or someone else's energy or upset the equilibrium of energy in the Universe. Fluctuation from high to low is not necessary. Highs and lows are based on the idea that there is a ceiling. Therefore, in order for the ebb and flow of life to occur, there must be a floor. That is not so. On an energy level, when the limit is reached, that limit then becomes the base from which we shoot for the next limit. So the ebb and flow is an ever expansive movement. In terms of the life force, each of us puts more knowledgeable, aware energy back into the system via our experience and learning. Even if the learning and experience appear negative, they are absorbed on the energy level as growth. For example, perhaps our experience with war and violence is teaching us on an energy level about the futility of war and violence. Therefore, people being born out of that consciousness are increasingly aware on the deepest level of their beings that they must find another way. We do not learn intellectually. It seems we must all make the same mistakes and have difficulty profiting from the mistakes of others. However, on an energy level, we do learn, and our learning goes into the stream of consciousness to purify, cleanse, expand our awareness and evolve our souls. Our evolution is infinitely slow, but we are evolving.

If I understand that I cannot steal energy from you without stealing energy from me, war is truly futile. If I also understand that shortages are due to my state of awareness and evolution, and are not the reality, I don't need to steal. I am not less because of you; I am less than what I want to be only because of my state of awareness, and that I can change. Thus, you are no longer my enemy. My ability to have is curtailed only by my lack of imagination and my ability to receive. If I keep my vision focused on what I want, my intuitive processes will show me how to get it. There is no way anyone can prevent me from getting what I want if I follow the natural law.

I. Each person gets what he needs. You may not be where you want to be at this point in time, but you are where you need to be to learn whatever it is you have to learn in order to get what you want and enjoy it.

J. You cannot err. If the individual is in perfect equilibrium based on awareness of and commitment to his own internal rhythm, then he is also in perfect equilibrium with the rhythm of the Universe around him. How is it possible to make a mistake when you are totally at one with the Universal ebb and flow? There is no way to lose or to miss anything. All is available to you on that level.

K. We each have access to all the energy there is. This is the essence of the maxim that we are all created equal. Each of us, via the route of our intuitive, feeling processes, has access to all knowledge and awareness.

L. There are no limits. In metaphysical literature there are many descriptions by different individuals of their "out of body" experiences.* If we can learn to travel beyond the limits of the physical body, then what is to stop us from traveling through the Universe just by understanding the energy processes which would transport us there? This was the premise put forth by Richard Bach in his recent best-selling book.* Remember how Jonathan learned to transport himself by letting himself imagine where he wanted to be, and suddenly he was there?

Our scientists have been experimenting for some time with telepathy—the ability to communicate over distance without words or machines. Already, limits we have presumed absolute are falling before our eyes. I think this is only the beginning. As we let go of our need for limits, the possibilities open to us are truly beyond our wildest dreams.

---

* Most recently, Robert Monroe, *Journeys Out of the Body*.
* Richard Bach, *Jonathon Livingston Seagull*. MacMillan.

10
The Evolution
of the Individual

AS I MENTIONED EARLIER, it is vital for an individual to have a strong internal structure (sense of self) in order to handle the intensity of the energy flowing in and through him when he moves into expanded levels of consciousness. I think that the following are the necessary ingredients of that structure:

A. Survival shift and the elimination of addiction. Many people function as though they are addicted to someone or something external to themselves. They behave as though that person, job, or place is the reason for living. The individual feels he is not a whole person without his mate, and he builds his life around that person. If anything happens to that relationship, he cannot work, sleep, think, or perform his everyday tasks. He bases his sense of security and comfort in the world on that relationship. Without that person, he feels afraid, off balance, and immobilized.

Some people are addicted to sex. The individual has to have his "fix" at regular intervals. It doesn't much matter who the sexual partner is. Such an individual uses the sensation as a security blanket. It alleviates his tension, fear, upset, and keeps him from feeling alone with whatever terror that state holds for him. Still others use food in this way, or alcohol or drugs. Whatever the object, the process is the same. The individual believes he will fall apart without that object, and he devotes a great deal of energy toward making sure his particular addictive object is always available to him.

Now, there is nothing necessarily wrong with an addicition. In fact, most people use their addictions as a form of grounding. As long as an individual focuses his energy on a person, place or thing, that obsession keeps him alive and prevents his giving up in despair. For example, remember Scarlett O'Hara's devotion to her family plantation, Tara in *Gone With the Wind?* In the last scene of the first half of the picture, just before the intermission, you see her standing on the ravaged land of her former home. She is in rags and covered with grime as she looks toward heaven and swears to restore her home to its former beauty. It is a powerful scene because it is clear that her blind devotion to that dream enables her to maintain her sanity in the face of the devastation she is experiencing.

In my profession as therapist, I have seen many people use marriage in this way. Not infrequently, individuals will suicide after the break-up of a marriage, not because of the marriage, but because they are using the marriage to cover some deep pain or depression that really did not have to do with the marriage. Other people will focus their energy on making money or saving the world. Many therapists fall in the latter category. As long as they can focus on other people's pain or problems, they don't have to deal with their own which may feel overwhelming to them.

Some people base a sense of well-being on an ability to control the environment. As long as everything and everyone are predictable, they feel comfortable. However, if someone rocks the boat, they panic.

Many people are able to attach a sense of security and comfort to someone or something external to themselves, and that arrangement works quite satisfactorily for them, at least for awhile. They provide themselves with a type of secure, stable nest which makes it possible for them to develop parts of themselves they might not otherwise explore. However, if the individual chooses to go in the direction of the development of his intuitive and feeling levels of consciousness, the addictions have to go. The reason for this is that the energy it takes to maintain the addiction is so great that it does not leave enough space for the individual to pursue these other levels. How can you stay in your house and write poetry when there is a riot in the street, or how can you worry about saving your soul when you are starving to death? The exploration of the feeling, intuitive level takes everything we have, and the maintenance of whatever external we are addicted to also takes everything we have. The two are not compatible. So, if the individual begins to move in the direction of exploring his feelings and letting his feelings and intuition take the lead in his life, he will eventually be confronted with a choice. He will, without even being aware of it, continually put himself in situations in which his addiction is challenged. For example, a couple came to see me because they were unable to make a decision about their relationship. They had been together two years and during that time had made several decisions to split which they always reversed. They couldn't seem to live with each other, and they couldn't live without each other. At the time they came to see me, they had once more decided to live together and resolve their situation one way or the other, but each was feeling frustrated and confused. The basis of their difficulty was that he felt she was constantly withholding her feelings from him. She said she loved him, but he never felt she let go and committed herself to the relationship. She felt that whenever she took a stand for herself with him, he would get hurt and become angry and judgmental. I then asked him what he was learning by being with a woman whom he experienced as withholding; and what was she learning by being with a man who responded to her assertions with hurt, anger, and judgments. As we explored those questions, he realized that when a woman was important in his life, he had always given her the power to validate him. If she loved him, then he was worthwhile in terms of how he felt about himself. If she rejected him, then he was devastated because it meant there was something basically wrong with him. However, she constantly had to prove that she loved him by doing what he wanted her to do. If she did not give what he wanted when he wanted it, then she did not love him. He was now with a woman who said she loved him, but who withheld from him. However, she didn't leave him, either. So the relationship threw him off balance. She didn't love him, according to his previous standards about what love meant, but neither did she leave him, which made it difficult for him to convince himself that she really didn't love him. I offered to him that being with her was forcing him to learn how to take his power back to himself in terms of being the judge of his own worth. If he could learn to do that with her, he could do it with anyone. That meant he could allow her to be whoever she was without using her responses or lack of responses to evaluate himself.

She realized that, because he wouldn't let go and was continually pushing her for what he wanted, he was forcing her to assert. She recognized that, not only had she never committed herself to a relationship, she had never committed herself to her own feeling. She always held back a part of herself. She never let go totally into joy, sadness, anger, or anything else she was feeling. She would go just so far in expressing herself and then pull away.

I indicated that, separate from what they felt about the relationship, each of them was currently using the other to break his own addiction. If she could assert her feelings and her limits to him, she could do it with anyone. His way of expressing his anger and hurt triggered her guilt, and his consistent pushing made it impossible for her to withdraw because he wouldn't take withdrawal for an answer. So, she was confronted with a situation in which she could either leave or change. Since she wasn't leaving, it was evident that she was ready to change. I indicated that obviously they had chosen each other well because each was dealing with the same process in terms of his growth, and neither was a quitter—each was determined to "hang in there" until something got resolved.

I think that the part of the individual's consciousness which is directing his growth (not the cognitive part) will drive him to break his addictions when he is ready to let go. The reason for that is that the highest expression of creativity is based on the development of the intuitive, feeling aspects of consciousness. Creativity is dependent on the individual's ability to express his uniqueness through whatever avenue is most appropriate to him. Uniqueness cannot be expressed by conformity, imitation, or repression. The experience of one's own uniqueness is entirely dependent on the individual's awareness of his own particular rhythm.

I offered to the couple I described above that they were ready to break their addictive structures in order to experience the creative part of themselves. Also, it was necessary to break the addictive structures in order to go more deeply into their experience of intimacy. On an energy level, it is possible to move inside another person and experience his feelings as though they were your own. However, it is vital in this process to have a strong enough sense of your own identity that you do not lose awareness of yourself in this powerful process. If I keep asserting my feelings and you keep asserting yours—neither of us holds back—we will move into this level. However, we will sabotage it in some way if we cannot maintain our separateness in that experience. It is as though I can merge my spirit with yours, but I am always aware that I am me, feeling your energy and your feelings; I do not experience that your feelings are my own.

This is one of the reasons that couples often have violent fights or withdrawal behaviour following their most intense experience with each other. The intensity triggered a warning that each was not yet clear enough in his sense of himself to maintain that level of interaction without a loss to himself, so he must retreat to develop his self-awareness more explicitly. That sense of self is determined by my awareness on all levels of consciousness that I am in charge of myself. If I have any doubts that I am in charge of my own worth, I will not even go to that level. Very often, couples will find that, at the point in their relationship where they have developed the greatest understanding and closeness, some seemingly insoluble problem emerges that really shouldn't even be that important. Usually, it is not the issue that is important. What is happening is that their inability to resolve the issue is a clue that they are ready to go to a new depth in their relationship but must do further work on developing themselves more individually. Deep intimacy requires a strong sense of boundaries—I must know what my limits are and that I can say no even at the risk of losing you. I must be able to hear or experience your feelings and, at the same time, be aware of and able to respond with my own. I must feel so clear about who I am that I can always differentiate between you and me no matter how much I abandon myself to my experience in the moment with you.*

B. Replacement of the addictive structure with a structure based on the positive flow of energy, totally devoid of negativity. When an individual lets go of defining himself around another person, object, performance, or place, he does not automatically have something to take its place. The energy it takes to hold onto something takes up the space both inside and around the individual. When he lets go, he leaves a space for new energy to emerge, either from inside or outside of himself. How often have you heard someone say, "I met a new friend when I stopped stewing over whether or not I would ever meet a new friend!" Or, you quit a job you couldn't stand and didn't have any idea what you wanted to do. Then an ad in the paper caught your eye, or a friend called out of the blue and suggested something. Most of us have had the experience of letting go in some way on the inside and then suddenly finding something new. That is not a coincidence—it is an energy phenomenon.

---

* Luthman, *Intimacy.*

For most people, the experience of limbo that occurs when you let go is very frightening. We feel off balance because there is nothing around which to mobilize. We are more comfortable when there is pain or difficulty because at least we can mobilize our resources and *do* something. I think that off-balance position is the most difficult growth process to experience for most of us because we are so used to feeling alive and worthwhile only when we are mobilized. The reality is, however, that that limbo place is extremely valuable. On an energy level, that is the space in which we let go, experience the loss, and prepare for the next stage of development. It is a savoring place, a preparation place, a resting place. It is the ebb aspect of our rhythm. As we learn to trust it and wait for new direction to emerge, we become more comfortable with it so that, instead of feeling off balance, we have a sense of self as a buoy on water—bouncing, going nowhere in particular externally, but not in jeopardy.

I experienced myself in that limbo during my sabbatical, after I had finished my second book. It was very difficult for me to stay in that experience because it was the first time in my life when I did not have a goal—something I was shooting for, looking forward to, mobilizing myself to achieve. I felt totally off balance. At times I would panic, and I used meditation to restore calm. At other times I would try to move in a new direction, and something would occur which would block my effort. Most of the time, I simply did not have the interest or energy to do anything. I was baffled at first because I wasn't depressed, I wasn't sick, I didn't have a particular problem to work on. I was just there, feeling as though the past was unimportant and the future non-existant—what an experience! I was in that limbo for four months, and as I got less afraid and more familiar with the experience, I realized that a great deal was going on internally. A lot of things were coming together for me inside of myself. In that process, I said goodbye to the use of suffering as a way of growing and learning, and I made a commitment to trust myself totally and go in the direction of what made me happy and alive. When that commitment had permeated all levels of my being and felt solid to me, a direction began to emerge. The first step was a desire to form the beginning group which I described to you in my first chapter.

C. Nature of the Energy Structure: 1) Unconditional love— everything we do is done for the purpose of facilitating growth, of learning something we would not learn any other way. The process we use to learn may be destrucive, depreciating or restrictive, but it is the best method we have at our command at the moment. This may be because we are at an early stage of evolution, or because there is a wide gap between our expanded levels of consciousness and the cognitive level. Therefore, the intuitive level has to use crude means to get through to us since we do not perceive nuances. For example, a woman came in to see me feeling as though there was something terribly wrong with her because she had been living with a man for the past five years whom she thought was very depreciating in his behavior toward her. Yet she stayed in the relationship and couldn't make herself let go of him. I asked her what positive changes she had noticed in herself in the past five years. She thought for awhile and then said she had become increasingly assertive and had taken risks she never thought possible for herself. She had always been shy and retiring, but .in the last few years she had begun to reach out to other people more, had joined some groups, and this year had even decided to go back to school. I asked what triggered all of this, and she indicated that her boredom and frustration with the man she mentioned had given impetus to her risk-taking. He was the kind of person who did one thing and said another. As a result, she could never depend on him and was constantly thrown back on her own resources. I suggested that perhaps that was why she continued to be connected to him. While he wasn't the person she wanted, and his lack of appreciation and irresponsibility were painful to her, her relationship with him was pushing her into areas of growth. Apparently, on some level of her consciousness, that growth was more vital to her than the pain and discomfort she had to experience to achieve it. I suggested that she begin to focus on how the relationship was contributing to her growth rather than what was wrong with her for staying in it. If she could do that, then perhaps she would open up a way to learn to continue her growth via a means that was more enjoyable and less hurtful to her. Several weeks later she terminated the relationship and indicated that, although she felt lonely, she also felt relieved and ready to let go.

When I indicated that she was staying in the relationship, not because she was sick, but because she was learning something vital to her growth in it, that awareness freed her to make a choice—to stay with him for further learning or to leave and continue her learning in another situation—without any loss to her self-esteem. You can see the same process in an external situation with a child. When you tell him he has to do something because it is the good or right thing to do, he will often rebel and fight you. If you give him a choice—he can either stop fighting with his brother or be put in his room for a half hour because you can't stand the noise—the situation will usually resolve itself very quickly, particularly if past experience has indicated you will follow through. The difference is that the choice leaves him in control, and, either way he goes, there is no damage to his self-esteem. If he gives in, it is because he doesn't want to go to his room. If he doesn't give in and gets put in his room, it isn't because he is wrong or bad but because you don't like the fighting at that moment.

The same process is internalized. When I realize that what I am doing does not make me wrong or bad but is a way of learning, then I am free to decide whether I need to learn the hard way or whether there is an easier way for me to discover myself. I either have to risk asserting my feelings, even though that will take me into unknown, unpredictable territory, or I can continue to stay in a situation that will force me to assert until I can do it without being pushed. When I take the judgments off myself, there is nothing to rebel against, and I am free to decide on the basis of the best learning route for me at the time.

2) The individual takes responsibility for *everything* that happens to him without judging himself, trying to alter his behavior, depreciating himself, or trying to analyze the situation. He does not even have to *believe* that he is responsible. All he has to do is consider the possibility that some aspect of himself is contributing to the situation for purposes of teaching him something. If he opens his mind to this possibility and it is so, the answer will come to him intuitively. It may not come the moment he asks, but it will come. If nothing comes to him, and he continues to feel that the situation is not of his making, then he has lost nothing. One can only gain by the exploration. The process of just confronting oneself with this possibility opens up the channel of communication between the intuitive levels of consciousness and the cognitive level since the intuitive level is then receiving appreciation and recognition for its true nature.

3) The individual takes responsibility for choosing the parents and family to whom he was born. It is not important whether or not you believe this. Just pretend that you chose your parents and your particular family situation to develop some aspect of your consciousness, and then consider what that might be. The minute you consider this possibility, even in pretense, you automatically take yourself out of the victim role. Suddenly you are no longer defined in relation to the kind of parents you had. You are you, and you utilized your experience with them to modify, polish, expand, develop certain parts of yourself.

As a therapist, one of the things that has always perturbed me was the fact that we helped clients to the point of understanding and experiencing their feelings about their problems in relation to their parents, but it seemed to me we left them there. Somehow the parents are eternally the bad guys. Even if we forgive them, the act of having to forgive still makes them responsible. If we consider that we chose them with all their faults, what is there to forgive? Obviously we needed them to be exactly the way they were, with all their faults and assets, in order to learn what we needed to know. And, if they had not been available, we would have chosen others with the same or similar ways of being. Even though the possibility of such a choice may seem ridiculous, just the act of considering it puts you in charge of yourself in a way you probably have not experienced before.

4) Meditation is a vital component of the energy structure. It is the major tool by which the individual opens up his intuitive levels of consciousness. As the individual meditates, messages and direction will come to him from his intuitive self, and, if he acts on those messages and directions, he learns to trust them. The increase of trust opens up our inner resources even more. When you really trust another person and you feel that person trusts you, you will open up your deepest feelings to that friend. The same is true internally. The act of trusting the intuitive level of yourself opens up all the secrets and resources of that level.

Do not push yourself to meditate. If you try it and find you do not want to continue, then don't. Just file away the idea in your insides and do it when it fits you to do so. The reason for this is that meditation speeds up the opening of the channels between your intuitive level of consciousness and the cognitive level. You may not be ready to increase the speed of that opening. Trust your insides to let you know the pace that is appropriate for you. When I first started to meditate, I would do it for about fifteen minutes once a week. I increased it gradually, but not by an act of will. It just happened. Now, I usually meditate twice a day for thirty to forty-five minutes. It feels as necessary to me as food and water. People often ask me how to meditate. I feel it is appropriate to do it in whatever way is most fitting to you. I usually sit in a comfortable chair with my legs stretched out in front of me on a hassock and the palms of my hands on my legs. In that position, I feel contained and connected to myself, and I'm not in danger of going to sleep. Then, I have two different kinds of meditation that I use. They may not really be different, but I divide what I do into two parts because it fits me to do it that way. One part is a Yoga type meditation in which the purpose is to experience myself in a kind of suspended state. With my eyes closed, I focus on a spot of light between my eyes on the bridge of my nose and keep my focus there until I achieve a kind of detachment between my mind and body in which my head feels turned off. I am not thinking about anything. I am alert and am most aware of a sensation which feels timeless and motionless. I find that state very nourishing. In addition, it seems to restore my equilibrium. Anxieties and stresses disappear in that experience.

The other kind of meditation I use is what I call my active, working one. In that state, you can either talk to the other levels of yourself as though different aspects of your consciousness can communicate with each other, or you can talk to God if he is part of your belief system. The point is, you utilize the energy law that says you can create your own world. You picture what you want and then affirmatively thank your intuitive level, or God, for bringing that desire about. You assume that the demand is the same as the deed. I heal myself or others on that level by focusing on the person's image and picturing energy surrounding that person. I do exercises for expanding my consciousness. For example, if I hear a dog barking when I am meditating, I picture myself (not my body) going out to that dog, watching him bark, then merging with him to experience his barking from the inside. Books on meditation offer many such exercises as impetus, and you will soon develop your own.

If you would like to meditate but want a more formal structure, you can contact your local International Meditation Society. They will be listed in your phone directory under that title. They offer a short course in the art of meditation and provide you with a mantra (a phrase to assist you in getting into a deep state of awareness) upon graduation.

If you want to experiment on your own but want other ideas, find a Metaphysical book store and browse. Let your intuition be your guide and select those books on meditation that attract and interest you.

5) Explore everything from the positive framwork of expansion and receptivity rather than highs and lows, joy and depression. For example, if something happens to you that is upsetting, consider what it means in terms of what you are building rather than from the stand-point of what is wrong with you. One day when I was driving my car, a policeman stopped me for making a rolling stop at an intersec-tion. He didn't give me a ticket but did give me a warning. In the past I would have berated myself for making such a stupid mistake. This time I considered what it might be that my intuitive level was trying to warn me about. Immediately I realized that I had been allow-ing myself to vibrate to some depressed feelings that morning, and my intuitive level was saying to me, "Don't waste your time and energy—you don't have to do that anymore."

In another instance, I had been jogging for two miles every day. One day I injured my ankle slightly so that I could not run for several days. In the past I would have really been annoyed because I felt the exercise was good for me and having to take several days off broke my rhythm. It would take me several days to build up to my usual pace again. Instead of focusing on my loss, I again questioned what my intuitive level was saying to me. I realized later that I had subtly shifted my exercise program over time so that instead of it fitting whatever my body needed at any given point in time, the program had become an end in itself and something I was pushing my body to do whether it fit in the moment or not. I felt the slight injury was saying to me that I could set up goals, but that it was important that I be able to change them or let go of them if they didn't fit my natural rhythm at any point. If I stayed with my rhythm, all things would flow to me and from me in the most fitting way.

6) Translate your experience in relationships on the basis of

where you are in your unfolding development rather than in terms of pathology or judgment. In the past, I had difficulty comfortably letting go of a relationship unless I could diagnose what was wrong with the other person. Once I could justify to myself that the other person was manipulative, repressed, or infantile, then I could walk away, conscience clear, certain that my inability to relate to that person did not mean that something was wrong with me.

One of the most difficult shifts I have had to make was to learn how to perceive relationships without anyone being in the wrong. In my beginning attempts to explore expanding my consciousness and intuition, I talked to a number of psychics, mediums, and astrologers to ascertain if their direction was similar to my own. One evening I went to a lecture given by a woman who teaches meditation and parapsychology at one of the local universities. There were about seventy-five or eighty people at the meeting. I experienced ambivalence almost from the moment I entered the room. A part of me wanted to be there because I felt there was something I could gain from the lecture, but another part of me was uncomfortable. I didn't understand the reasons for either impulse, so I just stayed with my ambivalent feelings, trusting that they would eventually resolve themselves. As the lecture commenced, I noticed that I sat in a very closed position throughout, with arms and legs tightly crossed. I know from experience in my profession that our body language is very explicit, and we will frequently react on a physical level long before we are cognitively aware anything is going on. So, I've learned to be an observer of my own body clues as a way of getting in deeper touch with the intuitive aspects of my consciousness. I'll talk about that in more detail in a later chapter.

At one point, the lecturer asked the group to do some meditative exercises. I started to comply but felt so uncomfortable that I simply stopped and resumed my closed position. At a certain point in the lecture, I found myself saying, "Ah, that's what I came to hear," and I then felt ready to leave even though the meeting was not yet over. On the way home, I was aware that I was consciously stopping myself from going in the direction of using my reaction to put a negative evaluation on that group. Instead, I stayed with my sense of uncertainty and kept focusing on what that experience meant in terms of where I was in my growth. In the process, I realized that any time

I couldn't immediately put people and events in categories, I felt off balance. I was operating as though I had to make sense and order out of everything before I could move. In recognizing that, I appreciated that, up to now, my ability to do that had enabled me to develop a strong internal sense of who I am in relation to the world around me, but that process was currently getting in my way. It slowed me down and prevented me from flowing with my natural rhythm. I knew that my growth at this point required me to be able to trust my intuitive processes and move in whatever direction they pointed, even when it didn't make sense to me. Making people or situations right or wrong had been a way of taking me off my uncomfortable, off-balance position. The minute everything and everyone got categorized, my world was again right-side up.

As I allowed myself to stay off balance in this instance, I realized that everyone in that room was in a very different stage of development in terms of his intuitive awareness and the intensity of his energy level. By that I mean that as we trust our intuitive processes more, the amount of energy available to us increases. When the energy flow is unblocked, the individual has unlimited energy available to him from other sources around him, and his own internal energy is constantly intensified. Now, each person in that room was in a different stage of development in this respect. In addition, each person was in a different stage of development in terms of his sense of himself. All were obviously beginning explorers in this new realm. Therefore, many were out of balance with themselves, letting go of an old way of being and not yet clear about a new framework for handling this kind of expansiveness and energy. As a result, I experienced the energy in the room as chaotic and somewhat frantic. Because I was still unsure of my own balance, I had to protect myself from too much input. Therefore, no one was wrong or bad or toxic. All of us were simply too much out of synchronism with each other to be comfortable. I still was glad I went to the meeting because I learned about that process as well as got some information from the lecturer that was important to me. However, I realized that I would have to pace myself in frequenting those kinds of meetings because there was an energy cost to me to consider.

7) In the energy framework crying purifies other levels of consciousness, sexuality expands and intensifies consciousness, and

laughter provides balance and integration. We are constantly bombarded with negative energy in the form of fear, vindictiveness, and hopelessness. Its source may be other levels of our own consciousness which we are still in the process of expunging, the vibrations of other people around us, and negativity passed down through generations. I remember when I was a child that church scholars always seemed to have a difficult time explaining the Biblical declaration that the sins of the fathers are visited on the children. Now I begin to understand, in non-religious terms, that admonition.

If we are all aspects of a universal energy system, then whatever negative energy is transmitted into the system could survive beyond a particular concrete life span of the individual who transmitted it. It might dissipate in time, but it could continue in the system until it dissipated or until others in the system took conscious charge of the process of expunging the negativity. Therefore, I believe that each of us is carrying such negativity in his consciousness. As we begin the process of recognizing we can create our own world, and we begin to do so by vibrating to what we want, then the negativity rises to the surface. It is as though we are finally in charge of ourselves enough to be able to see it and deal with it without being overwhelmed.

Along this line, my first reaction to the Watergate expose was one of relief. I thought, "We are finally strong enough and grown-up enough to bring everything out into the open." I do not think that disclosure would have occurred unless we were ready, in an evolutionary sense, to take responsibility for the negativity we have created without being totally overwhelmed. We created the forms into which Nixon and his ilk fit by vibrating to fear, suspicion, and hatred of each other. As someone in one of my classes punned, "Nixon was impeached for our sins." Not that he is not responsible for his own process and involvement, but we created the climate into which he rose to eminence.

Now, my experience has been that, as my sense of myself and the intensity of the energy flow within and through me builds, I absorb less of the negativity around me. It is as though the power of my own energy structure is such that it creates an invisible shield against which negative energy bounces but does not penetrate. I have the most difficulty when the negative energy is coming from someone whom I love and to whom I am deeply committed. When that person is vibrating to intense anxiety, catastrophic fear, repression or vindictiveness, I often do not choose to walk away. I do not feel helpless as I used to when I knew someone I loved was suffering and there was nothing concrete I could do to change the situation. Now I recognize that each person has his own evolutionary journey and is working out some aspect of that journey even when he is in a situation that looks destructive or futile to me. In addition, I feel I can assist just by being there because, when my energy is flowing freely, I believe it has a healing effect on those around me without my having to do or say anything.

However, in this process I may absorb the other person's pain as though it was my own. If I understand this, then I can allow myself the luxury of tears as a cleansing mechanism without having to relate them to a particular event or problem. Other methods of cleansing include exercise and showers. How often have you felt depressed, then gone for a bicycle ride or a swim and somehow felt lighter. Or, perhaps you've had a difficult day, come home and taken a long shower, and felt the tension ease out of you as the water flooded over you. These experiences are not just external. On an energy level, there is a cleansing effect. Crying is the most powerful cleanser, however, and if we understand this, perhaps we can allow ourselves more release in this manner.

The sexual act gives impetus to the expansion of the intuitive levels of consciousness. I think this is why there have been so many taboos about sex and so many problems associated with sexuality. The orgasm is the one human experience in which it is impossible not to *be* the experience. You cannot be an observer watching yourself have an orgasm. In that experience, you are one with the energy flowing in and around you. That total release opens you up to data from your other levels of consciousness. Memories, old experiences, images, unresolved feelings—all suddenly have access to the cognitive level of yourself. If you are not prepared to be open to that data, you may react by becoming depressed, closing off, taking distance from your partner, or simply not letting yourself have a total experience at all.

Because of this phenomena, people who get involved sexually very early in the relationship take a risk. The sexual contact opens up their expanded levels of consciousness which may not coincide with where they are on a concrete level. As a result, one or both may get frightened and cut the relationship off suddenly, or they may experience intense feeling triggered by the opening up of those levels and then find that, as the relationship progresses on a concrete level, the feeling disappears. What has happened is that the relationship has gotten out of balance. Each does not have his sense of self balanced with his intuitive awareness, so he is thrown out of kilter by the intensity of the relationship on an energy level. Also, the connection on other levels of consciousness may not be supported by where each is on the concrete level, and the feeling may not sustain. For example, an individual may be extremely sensitive, intuitive, tender, and loving in the more expanded levels of himself. However, on a concrete level, he may not trust those parts of himself and is more rigid, logical, suspicious, and judgmental in his behavior. Now, in the sexual experience on an energy level, his or her partner may experience the more flowing aspects of his consciousness and be puzzled that the other person's words or behavior do not support the feeling experience. Most of you, I'm sure, have had such experiences. You have had moments of contact that seemed magical, and then the other person denies that such feeling existed or depreciates the power of it. Now, you are not imagining things. The power between you was real. However, the inability on the part of one or both of you to validate the power of that feeling in your words or behavior is a statement about the balance between your sense of self and your intuitive awareness, individually and between you in the relationship.

If people understand this phenomenon, then they can make a choice whether they want to get sexually involved right away and risk throwing themselves out of balance, trusting the balance to re-assert itself, or they can choose to build the relationship on the concrete level first and fit the sexual behavior to that framework. What people will do then, I think, will depend on how much pain is involved for them in opening up the expanded levels of consciousness in a relationship and then losing the relationship because they don't have the base to sustain that experience. The important thing is they don't have to make the decision based on what is right or wrong and they don't have to use the experience as an invalidation of their worth if it doesn't work out.

The ability to let go into laughter has a stabilizing and integrating effect. On an energy level, laughter itself or the awareness of the humor in a difficult situation has the effect of opening up perception of alternative choices. When one can see the ludicrous aspects of a dilemma, he is temporarily free of fear. On an energy level, the dissolution of fear always opens up that part of the individual which does have the answers on an intuitive level of self. Humor clears the channels which fear and anxiety block.

8) When an individual is beginning his journey into trusting his intuitive processes, it is important that he protect himself from energy that is negative or intrusive. Usually people do this by distancing themselves from others. During my sabbatical, I spent a great deal of time alone or with people whom I was sure would support my process without question. Gradually, as I felt stronger and more sure of myself, I was moved to test out my ideas on a wider and wider audience.

In the beginning of this process, however, old defenses are breaking down, and we don't have a new structure immediately to take the place of the old. In addition, because we are just starting to trust the intuitive level, energy is only beginning to get unblocked and is, thus, easily drained or intruded upon in this embryonic stage. As we progress, the energy level reaches such an intensity that it forms a much more powerful defense than any rigid external structure or way of being. As we get in touch with our own natural rhythm and a sense of how it meshes with the rhythm around us, we have our own built-in radar or sonar. We get vibrations, long before we reach a danger point, which tell us to change direction. As we tune into and trust the intuitive level, we become aware of the slightest nuance or clue that tells us we may be somewhat off the track. As the trust in our equilibrium, based on rhythm, builds, we develop increased awareness about other aspects of our being—esp, precognition, telepathy, heightened sensitivity to color, sound, and smell. With such expansion comes a strong sense of power and the gradual elimination of any fear or anxiety. Thus the flow of energy through us becomes increasingly powerful—so powerful, I think, that not only does it prevent the absorption of negative energy, but it purifies other energy that comes into our atmosphere. Thus, I feel we can heal just by being in the same room with another person, without having to do or say anything. Have you even been with a group of people who were all feeling high and expansive when you were depressed? After awhile, you find that you either have to let go of your depression to be with them or to leave them in order to hold onto your depression. You cannot maintain the depression in the face of their positive energy.

11
The Overview

I WOULD LIKE TO SHARE my concept of the individual's overall evolutionary journey. I believe that the individual, on a pure consciousness level, is perfect. The evolutionary process does not consist of an imperfect organism progressing toward wholeness. It involves the expunging of layers of negativity and distortion so that the wholeness can be revealed. Also, in the expunging process, the consciousness is expanded by the experience. So, the evolutionary process involves the dissolution of whatever limitations are in the way toward our awareness of perfect consciousness and the utilization of that dissipation process for the purpose of expanding the excitement and creativity of the consciousness.

Therefore, the evolutionary process is not linear—in a straight direction chronologically. There is no time, no past or future. Everything is happening right now. We use the chronological concept because it gives us a concrete framework which is easier for us to grasp. That is all right; however, it is limiting, and at some point, when we are ready, we will have to give it up. Say, for example, that you are like a television set. At this point in your awareness you are tuned in to channel four, which is your conscious awareness of your life now. You are evolving that aspect of your being most evident in this particular channel. However, there are, say, thirty other channels operating at the same time. If you flip the dial, you will tune in to another channel, but channel four is still going on with its program. I believe that consciousness works in a similar way. If I knew the processes for doing it, perhaps I could shift and see myself as another person at another place in time or history, developing another aspect of my consciousness in that experience. I could be a black slave in 1840, experiencing what it is like to be downtrodden and brutalized, so that, on an energy level, I can expunge myself of any desire to achieve growth in that way, knowing that the brutalization of anyone results in the lessening of everyone. I could then flip to another channel and see myself traveling in space in 2050, beginning to experience the vast potential open to me, unlimited by war, deprivation, or disease. Another channel might reveal me as a nineteenth century woman dedicated to family and home, experiencing that aspect of my personality in depth and detail. Still another channel might reveal me as a crippled beggar on the streets of an Asian country, struggling, on an energy level, to develop that aspect of my consciousness which has been insensitive to the pain and suffering of others. On another change of the dial, I might be a wealthy nabob totally absorbed in a hedonistic pursuit as a way of learning that sensuality is meaningless without a spiritual balance.

I suspect we are not limited by body or space. If we opened our minds to the possibility that all the limitations we accept may not be valid, we might discover that we could transport ourselves anywhere we wanted to go as pure energy. I do a meditation exercise in which I see myself shooting through space, seeing vast areas of atmosphere with stars and planets and other universes all around me. Periodically, I look back and see my body maintaining itself in a meditative position, waiting for me to return. I wonder if I can take the next step so that I *am* that experience, not just myself imagining that I am having that experience. I do believe that is the next step. What we imagine becomes real when we are prepared for that to be so.

If, then, there are no limitations, and time is an illusion, so are our concepts of aging, illness, and death. Perhaps we age according to our expectations rather than according to hard and fast dicta. If, after conception, tiny brain cells determine the formation of arms, legs, fingernails, et cetera, then why couldn't we still grow new arms, legs, teeth, or whatever we may lose, if we knew how to trigger those same cells into action? What if death as we know it is an illusion? Suppose that death is a statement that we have finished whatever we needed to learn about this aspect of consciousness and are shifting to another level. That level may be another channel, as I discussed before, or it may be a level based on pure energy without a concrete manifestation. There may be many different types of environments in which we develop. Science fiction writers have delighted us for years with vivid imaginings about such possibilities. Perhaps their imaginations were in touch with other realities which we are not yet ready to recognize cognitively as real.

I feel that, as a race, we are about to make a shift, letting go of suffering as a way of learning, to growing by means of expansiveness through the experience of oneness with each other and all energy around us. This means that we are beginning to focus on aliveness rather than power, security, or sensation as our meaning for living. As we open up our awareness, we develop a sensitivity to our connection with all of life. It is difficult to ravage the earth or kill an animal for no reason when we experience the earth or that animal as part of ourselves.

In my personal growth, I shifted my survival and aliveness from a judgmental structure of right and wrong to a structure based on growth. The basis of that structure was the assertion of feelings and trust that whatever was fitting to my feelings and facilitated my experience of growth was healthy for me and beneficial to others. The next and most difficult shift was to recognize that nothing I did was wrong; I could make no error; everything I did was for the purpose of growing and learning whatever it was I needed to know in order to realize my greatest desires. I think that, on a universal consciousness level, the whole race is in the same process. We are very close to giving up war, disease, and the deprivation. We have about reached a point where we have learned all we can by those means. Now we have to find other ways. Those ways have to do with learning via excitement, aliveness, and unlimited personal power. The basis of that learning is the awareness that it is possible for me to be both serene and joyous *all* of the time. Those states are not dependent on external phenomena. They are not even dependent on my dying and reaching some magical place called heaven or achieving some kind of Nirvana via a denial of this worldly experience. In my pure consciousness is the awareness of joy and peace—I must travel until the barriers in the way to my experience of that level of myself are dissolved. No one else will do it for me, nor can I escape that task. The sooner I accept that reality, the more exciting and less tedious my journey.

I believe that with the acceptance of that reality on all levels of consciousness there is an end to suffering. The journey from that point on is characterized by perfect health and increasing joy. The individual becomes aware that when he is not joyous he is slightly off course, and that awareness becomes his subtle master, holding him gently to a smooth and trouble-free path. We do not have to have trauma and pain and problems to provide excitement and keep life from being boring. The experience of the drug culture has given us a taste of the treasures available to us. The experiences of people on mind-expanding drugs have given us a glimpse of what is possible with the expansion of consciousness. The world becomes many-dimensional, and we realize we have only skimmed the surface in our exploration thus far. My experience is that people who take conscious charge of the development of their expanded levels of consciousness go far beyond what can be accomplished on any drug. This is because the individual is in balance and can keep building on his experience. Drugs can precipitate a great opening of consciousness and just as great a closing when they wear off. Or they may result in a scattered, chaotic effect similar to what we see in the process we label as psychotic. Some people have used drugs to give impetus to the opening of consciousness and then been able to use that opening to build on and move past any need for the drug. Therefore, while some people may utilize drugs to facilitate their growth, they will reach a point at which the drug becomes a limiting factor rather than an assistance. So drugs, like everything else, are neither good nor bad in the overall view.

As you develop your energy framework, you will find that automatically you become a healer. Intense, free-flowing energy *does* heal. When my partner and I taught in Amsterdam, I visited the famous Dutch psychic, Gerard Croiset.* He has successfully assisted the police in the solution of many cases through the utilization of his esp abilities, and he holds healing sessions in his home for all who would come. He gave me a demonstration of his healing phenomenon by passing his hands over my body about four inches from the skin surface. I could feel intense heat. He is unable to explain this occurrence except to say that he has always had such ability. I believe that we all are capable of developing it and automatically do when we expand consciousness.

In the Bible there is a story about Jesus walking through a crowd.

---

* Jack Harrison Pollack, *Croiset, the Clairvoyant.* Bantam Books, 1961.

Suddenly he stopped and asked who had touched him. Everyone was surprised because in such a crowd there were obviously many people jostling each other. He said that it was a special kind of touch because energy had gone out of him. Later a woman came forward saying she had touched the hem of his garment because she wanted to be healed, and she thanked him for healing her. I suspect that Jesus was a highly evolved soul who was a vessel for the transmission of the kind of intense energy that is available to all of us.

As you develop your awareness of yourself as an energy transmitter, you can consciously focus it, particularly via meditation, on whomever you want to heal. I do it by picturing the person with light enveloping him or by picturing him *becoming* whole and healthy. I think that the imagery, plus the assumption that such energy can heal, produces the desired effect. I do not think that someone will be healed who is still utilizing the illness for purposes of learning, but I think that many times someone is ready to give up an illness and can use assistance in speeding up the process.

12
Racial and World Evolution

JUST AS THE INDIVIDUAL EVOLVES in the intensification of energy and the expansion of consciousness, so does the universal consciousness. (Let me re-assert here that I am not presenting these ideas as factual. I am simply using my imagination to trigger your own. I say this because I don't want you to cloud your perception with incredulity. I want you to let my ideas flow through you just to awaken your own vast store of knowledge on these other levels of consciousness.)

I see our total consciousness as an amorphous but intact amoeba. If you push it in in one place, it pops out in another. There is a homeostasis or balance. Thus, one individual cannot go past a certain point in his evolution and sustain it unless he has the support of the total group. We periodically generate a highly evolved individual who serves the purpose of being a harbinger, giving those who wish to see a symbol of what is to come. However, he then gets killed, like Jesus, isolated, or we make a God out of him which automatically absolves us from the responsibility that we could be just as evolved.

You can observe this principle of balance operating in your own family or marriage. Externally, if one child in the family is very outgoing, there is often another who is quite subdued. If someone in the family gets very upset, someone else will do or say something that calms things down. If one parent gets seriously ill, the children are cooperative and agreeable until the crisis is over; then all hell breaks loose. Notice that when your spouse gets hysterical you get very calm, and the reverse also occurs. Seldom do you both get hysterical at the same time. If that were to happen, the children or relatives or friends would provide a calming influence. We do not usually do this balancing act consciously or deliberately. There is a balancing mechanism on an energy level among people who are deeply committed that seems to have a life of its own.

I think the same mechanism operates on a racial and cultural level. One of the most obvious examples is the fact that the birth rate of males versus females never gets very far out of balance, and, when it does get at all out of balance, that phenomenon seems to coincide with what is happening historically. For example, the ratio of boy babies to girl babies usually increases during and following a war when the male population gets decimated. In the United States during the last fifteen or twenty years, the number of females of marriageable age has been somewhat larger than the number of males of like age. I think there may be a reason for this on an energy, evolutionary level. In the beginning of the history of this country, the majority of pioneers were men who spent much time alone in wilderness areas carving out new territory. On an energy level, that experience gave males learning in assertion, self-sufficiency, and risk-taking. During the same period, women were usually protected—going from the home of father to the home of a husband who continued as a buffer between them and the world. That protective environment enabled the female to develop her intuitive processes to a much greater degree than the male because all her energy was not caught up in sheer physical survival. However, her sense of power, ability to assert, and acceptance of responsibility for herself were extremely underdeveloped. A number of years ago Carl Jung said that man could not go further in his evolution until women came into their power. There had to be a balance.

With the shortage of men of marriageable age, more women have remained single or stayed single for a longer period than they might have if marriageable men were more plentiful. As a result, they have had more opportunity to develop their strengths, their assertive ability, and their powers. Now males in our culture are beginning to open up the intuitive aspects of their personalities. Increasingly, it is more acceptable for men to cry, to be artistic, to stay at home and take care of children, to abstain from fighting or hustling, without having their masculinity called into question. The balance universally is shifting to allow males and females to achieve balance within themselves individually between their intuitive and assertive elements. Thus, they do not have to use each other to make a whole—they must find other reasons for connecting with each other, other ways of being together that do not require either of them to repress any part of self.

I see many couples in therapy now who are experiencing the death of an old way of connecting and are confused about how to be with each other in a different way. For example, a couple I see now married when she was eighteen and he was twenty-five. He comes from an Italian heritage in which the man was reared according to "macho" tradition. He made the decisions, dominated his wife, was the boss and, in return, took care of her and protected her from the world. The wife came from a disrupted family in which there was little security and even less guidance. At the time of their marriage, she was grateful for his willingness to take over and tell her what to do and more than happy to define herself around him and whatever he wanted in return for such security and stability. However, during the ten years of their marriage, prior to their coming to see me, they had had two children, bought a home, and she had gone to work. In the process of mothering, taking care of the home, and achieving some success on her job, the wife had grown to the extent that she wanted to try her wings, make her own decisions and mistakes, learn about her own identity separate from a role as wife and mother. The husband, on the other hand, had begun to crack under the strain of always being the "strong" one who took all the heat, yet had no room to express sadness, uncertainty, or frustration. *Each* was ready for a change, so it was possible for a shift to occur and still maintain a balance. In addition, the culture as a whole is in a state of flux which supports such changes or, at least, does not actively sabotage them. It is now possible for people to live together without marriage, get a divorce, decide not to have children, live in a commune, or do a variety of other things without an avalanche of judgments and recriminations crushing them from without.

The problem for this couple was that, even though they wanted to change, it was difficult to let go of an old familiar way of being with each other for something they couldn't even see yet. They needed help in understanding that the old way could die, but it didn't necessarily mean that their marriage was dead. It did mean they would have to allow themselves to go into a kind of limbo in which they might feel estranged from each other in order to mourn the passing of the old and allow room for some new way of being with each other to emerge. I could not promise them that they could find a new way

of connecting, but I could assure them that if they did not fit wit
each other that realization would be evident to both of them on a
energy level and the decision to split would be a mutual one grow
out of equal awareness.

Another aspect of this phenomenon has to do with learning vi
energy channels. I believe that the expanded levels of our co
sciousness do have a memory bank and do learn by past experience
For example, there have been many periods of our history that hav
not repeated themselves. There is a rhythm of things done that car
and do not need to be done again. The artistic expression during th
Greek period was the ultimate moment of that kind of thing. It wa
as though the universal energy of that culture focused all of itse
on the highest forms of that aspect of expression to learn all that coul
be learned from that experience. Now as other aspects c
consciousness get equal time on an evolutionary basis, they ma
balance with that expression, and with the balance new height
may be reached at another time. However, it will be different becaus
the artistic expression will be in balance with all other aspects c
being.

Many people I know have expressed bitterness at their percep
tion that we seemed to have learned nothing from the slaughter c
six million Jews during the Second World War. We still have ant
Semitism and bigotry, oppression and murder, rationalized und
some ideology that suggests it is being done for our own good. A
of that is true. However, on an energy level, perhaps the energy th
was a part of those Jews who died returned to the system and is evol
ing now into concrete expression through the children coming int
being presently. If that is so, then they will have a deep aversion t
war and suppression of any kind. Without even knowing why, the
may not be able even to consider such acts. So war may be dissipate
out of our experience, not by logic, but by the deepest awarenes
on a consciousness level that it does not work. With that awarenes
we are forced to find other ways of being together.

In line with that concept, I believe that on an energy level th
Jewish culture has a highly evolved sense of oneness, commitmen
and responsibility in terms of their fellowman. However, that con
mitment which is their greatest achievement has within it the see
of their destruction in that they have sought to carry out that con

mitment by sacrifice rather than by commitment to aliveness. Their evolution as a culture is carrying them out of that sacrificial framework because they have learned, on an energy level, that sacrifice leads to destruction for everyone concerned. Now they are beginning to assert from a different framework based on self-respect and appreciation. They may have to over-kill for awhile in order to learn how to experience their own power positively. However, I don't feel that will last long because their commitment to life and the oneness of human consciousness is too strong. As they balance their commitment with love of self and seek to carry it out by taking responsibility for being totally alive, such exquisite balance will produce great power and beauty.

The philosopher, Rilke, has said, in effect, that we are not space traveling now because it would just be a matter of lugging guts from one planet to another. I agree. I think that our ability to travel in space freely will occur in balance with our ability to experience ourselves as one with everyone and everything around us. Another part of that balance will be our ability to experience strong emotion and deep intimacy with each other. Hermann Broch in his classic, *The Death of Virgil,* * expresses the idea that the only thing that will bring Virgil back from the brink of despair is deep emotion. Virgil had reached a point of wanting to die because he saw all human endeavor as totally inadequate. Broch makes the telling point that out of strong feeling comes the bridge back to human experience. This is true whether the individual is experiencing devastation at the death and destruction around him or awe at the magnitude and beauty of the Universe. In either place, he needs the ability to feel deeply and attach himself strongly to others to be grounded and in balance with such forces. Therefore, we will not go out into space on a vast scale, either concretely or in terms of expanded consciousness, unless that journey is balanced with an ability to love and be loved deeply and strongly with total commitment—no feeling held in reserve.

Broch also says that all man's earth experience is needed in the evolution of his soul. He must be ripped away from the earth (lose his addictions) or he remains earth-encrusted (chained to controlling his environment). However, he must return to experience earth from

* Hermann Broch, *The Death of Virgil.* Peter Smith.

a non-encrusted (non-addictive) state.* Man's ability to let go totally
into the experience of his sensuality is dependent on his faith that
the satisfaction of his soul is not dependent on a particular person
place or thing. It is dependent on his ability to be in charge of and
create his own world. When he accepts that he creates the forms
on an energy level, into which others are drawn who fit with him
then he does not have to use energy to hang on to anyone or anything
He can utilize all his energy to savor and explore the experience, know
ing that if that person or form leaves it is only because there is some
one or something better for him to take its place.

Therefore, the depth and breadth of exploration is balanced with
the depth of experience and of commitment to self.

In the evolution of the race, the contribution of the United States
has been the development of technology. We have carried that
development to the point of our own destruction. In order to prevent
that destruction, we are now forced back into the exploration and
development of ourselves so that technology does not control and
threaten us but can be balanced with a sense of oneness with each
other. Without that awareness, it is evident to the most blind of us
that we will use our knowledge against each other rather than for
the evolution of us all. That knowledge has gained a magnitude that
means total annihilation if utilized against each other. That is as far
as we will go in such development until we build a consciousness
base to handle more. Such is the nature of equilibrium.

Recently I saw a series of films on television that were made in
the 1920's. I was amazed at the rigid, judgmental framework of our
culture as reflected in those films. The message was clear that you
did your duty and that the focus of life was around honor, virtue, and
hard work. Feelings were obviously dangerous and to be repressed
and controlled at all times. We were basically animals who needed
to maintain rigid controls or we would destroy and be destroyed. I
suddenly became clear to me why the depression and the Second
World War occurred. Only such holocausts would have shaken us
loose from such a killing framework. The repression of feeling to that
extent produces a wooden, dead individual, family and culture.

In the sixties the balance tipped the other way with the drug

---

* Parenthesis, my interpretations.

scene, the riots at universities, and the other chaotic expressions of youth against a moralistc structure imposed on them from the outside against their wills. They spoke for all of us even though they may have been destructive to themselves and others in doing so. I believe the travesty of the Vietnam War and the exposure of the hypocrisy behind our moralistic facade during the Watergate scandals dealt the death blow to our suicidal tendency to "obey the rules" whether they made any sense or not and to give over responsibility for our behavior to someone or something beyond ourselves. We are now at a point where our salvation depends on our willingness to take responsibility to build a value structure which fits us, enables us to live together with understanding based on awareness of our oneness, and yet gives us room to change and grow without being locked into impossible expectations and demands.

During a recent meditation experience, I got a new insight into man's evolutionary journey in the story of Jesus and his death on the cross. We made him a God because that separated him from us and absolved us from the awareness that we could do everything he could do and more. However, he never gave any such message. On the contrary, he said over and over that we were the same as he and that the energy available to him was available to us. In that light, consider the possibility that his death on the cross (separately from your particular religious beliefs) symbolized the death of suffering. Suppose he was showing us that suffering could die, and that life did not have to consist of suffering unless we chose it to be so. His "resurrection" then was evidence of life without suffering. If that is so, then it has taken me two thousand years to see it, even though the message was clear and plain for all to see who would see. I do not experience that awareness as a criticism of myself, but only as an indication that it has taken over two thousand years for us to develop ourselves to the point that we may no longer need suffering as a means of learning. I can appreciate that it was necessary to get us where we are. I am overjoyed that I can see light at the end of the tunnel, and I know that beyond that light is beauty unchained and unmarred.

13
Survival of Positive Thought

I THINK THAT IN EVERY THOUGHT or system of belief that has survived, there is some universal truth related to energy laws and theory.

In the Catholic faith, purgatory is a state after death in which souls are purged and purified. The implication is that the soul is not yet ready for heaven and must expiate offenses committed in life so that it can be received into heaven. On an energy level the concept is removed from the idea of crime and punishment. In the book, *Seth Speaks,* Seth claims to be a personality from another level of consciousness who speaks through the writer, Jane Roberts, while she is in a trance-like state. He indicates that after death an entity frequently must have a limbo space in which he can let go of his illusions about life and death before he is ready to go on to his next evolutionary step. This is similar to the letting-go process I described earlier, in which an individual releases his hold on an old way of defining himself or an old way of connecting with other people and goes into a kind of limbo in which he mourns the loss of the old and prepares the way for the new. In the process of growth, we experience many little deaths because growth requires that we be able to let go of what no longer fits to make room for a new emergence.

The practice of confession is also a primary part of the Catholic religion. The purpose is to cleanse the soul and receive absolution for sins. On an energy level there is a similar process. In meditation the individual cleanses himself by expressing all those things about which he feels guilty and then appreciating that all of those acts were done for the purpose of learning something vital to his growth. That appreciation is a form of forgiveness which frees him from the necessity of repeating behavior which does not fit, because the appreciation opens up new channels of information from his other levels of consciousness. The act of confession, therefore, is similar in that it becomes a process of expunging negativity from the system. The atoning sinner feels unburdened and free of guilt.

If you separate the Bible from organized religion and read it from the standpoint of the growth model rather than judgment, it is a veritable treasure of energy principles. In the numerous references to Jesus' healing feats, he consistently taught that anyone who utilized his faith could do the same. The term faith really implies focusing your energy on an affirmative view of life. The concept of the oneness of universal consciousness is iterated many times—"As ye do unto the least of these . . . ye do unto me." Jesus said, "My kingdom is not of this world . . . ," which I think is a comment about letting go of addictions to achieve spiritual growth (expanded levels of consciousness). I think that teaching has been interpreted by some to mean denial of the world, but Jesus makes it very clear that there must be a balance between this world and any other—"Give unto Caesar that which is Caesar's . . . "

The concept of opulence—the ability to create a world devoid of suffering and rich in all that makes for aliveness—is repeated in at least thirty different verses in the New Testament, such as John 16:24, ". . . ask and ye shall receive, that your joy may be full . . ."

The idea that one cannot make an error when he is tuned in to his intuitive processes is implied in Romans—"All things work together for good . . . to those who are called according to his purpose." We are all unique expressions of the same energy—"There are diversities of gifts, but the same spirit . . ." I am isolating specific quotes, but if you read the whole book from this standpoint, you will begin to see the growth philosophy for yourself and to recognize that up to this time in our history we apparently needed to focus on the judgmental interpretation of the work rather than the energy concepts. I think that is a statement that we have not been ready, up to now, to move into that stratosphere. We needed the judgmental structure to hold us to earth until we could evolve to the point that we could utilize such potential.

In Buddhism part of the belief involves the transmigration of souls from lower to higher and back and forth. On an energy level I see that as similar to the concept that there are many aspects of consciousness in each of us and that it is possible to bring all of these aspects of ourselves into cognitive awareness through trust in our intuitive processes and the development of a sense of self based on ebb and flow. The idea of Nirvana, which I interpret as a state of perfection—total oneness with all around you, is comparable to the energy concept of the total perfection of consciousness, with evolution as the process of revealing that perfection.

Scientology, which is considered a philosophy by some and a religion by others, has a process inherent in the training of its members called clearing. As I understand it, the individual is assisted by the help of a trainer and a mechanical device to develop an awareness about what ideas and perceptions throw him off balance. The machine registers when he is upset, and an electrical impulse assists him to recognize his upset state and learn to experience the stimuli without losing his cool. This seems similar to the energy principle of vibrating to what is desirable and assuming that is your reality so that fear and doubt are dissipated.

I think that the basis of the whole field of science is that matter is energy, and energy cannot be created or destroyed but can be intensified and expanded. That is also the basis of the energy framework I have been discussing, with thoughts, feelings and ideas being considered as powerful energy sources.

In the field of metaphysics time is considered an artificial barrier, thoughts are energy, and there are energy laws which have to do with simple, impersonal cause and effect, not with crime and punishment.

The field of psychiatry and related sciences introduced us to the growth model and the relationship between sexuality and aliveness. Freud related all neurosis (unhealthy, symptom-producing personality structures) to the repression of sexual impulses, resulting in the individual's unclear sense of his own identity as male or female. Wilhelm Reich* narrowed this theory to relate all emotional illness to the repression of the bioenergetic function of the orgastic convulsion. He indicated that knowledge of the emotional functions of biological energy is indispensable for the understanding of its physical and physiological functions. He felt that the biological emotions which govern the psychic processes are themselves the direct expression of a strictly physical energy which he referred to as the cosmic orgone.

---

* Wilhelm Reich, *The Function of the Orgasm*. Farrar, Straus and Giroux, 1973.

My understanding is that both Freud and Reich put their emphasis on sexual energy (whether physical or psychic) as the source of health and aliveness. In the energy framework I have been discussing, it is vital for the individual to be strongly grounded in sensuality to achieve a balance with the development of his intuitive levels of consciousness. I include in the term sensuality the ability to form deep, intimate relationships as well as to savor sensual experiences. With that ability plus a solid intellectual structure of who he is, the individual can keep one foot solidly planted in this world and one in the next. With that foundation he can expand his other levels of consciousness and use that increased knowledge and perception to enhance his own evolution and that of others. The nature and character of his own energy is enhanced and strengthened, and he is more open for becoming a focal point through which the energy around him can focus with increased power and effectiveness because it is directed.

The concept of prevention has been a major contribution of the field of medicine. While much of the actual practice of medicine has been focused on meeting crisis and repairing damage, the research and the dream of many in the field has been on preventing disease by learning about optimum conditions for the maintenance of health. In the energy framework the consciousness is perfect, and as the individual gets in touch with his rhythm with increasing awareness of that consciousness, his body reflects his evolution. Thus, perfect health is an automatic boon accompanying reliance on the intuitive processes.

In the field of education the idea of structure has been developed to the point of rigidity because the form has become the reality into which everyone must fit, thus sacrificing the rhythm and flow necessary to the development of creativity. However, a structure is vital both to an individual and to a culture for continued expansion to occur. On an energy level, the emphasis is on the individual's development of his internal structure based on his sense of his unique rhythm and his awareness of who he is. With that solid internal structure he is then able to create external forms which fit his current stage of growth, but he is also able to let go of these forms to form other structures when the present ones lose their validity. Thus, his external environment moves and changes in synchronism with his internal flow.

We know from anthropological studies that all primitive cultures have explanations for death in which the common factor is that energy survives. In addition, all validate the power of sexual energy in that they all have rules to control or regulate sexual behavior.

The fields of philosophy and phenomenology are rich with energy concepts:

Goethe in "Faust" says that when man begins to create, terrifying total possibilities open up to him.

Rilke says that when we encounter each other at the intensity of which we are capable, that intensity commands change. On an energy level, it is impossible to stay around someone who is moving in the direction of expanded levels of consciousness without joining in the journey.

From James Agee's *Let Us Now Praise Famous Men* (1936):

> "For in the immediate world, everything is to be discerned, for him who can discern it, and centrally and simply, without either dissection into science or digestion into art, but with the whole of consciousness, seeking to perceive it as it stands: so that the aspect of a street in sunlight can roar in the heart of itself as a symphony, perhaps as no symphony can: and all of consciousness is shifted from the imagined, the revisive, to the effort to perceive simply the cruel radiance of what is."*

> Scheler: "This new attitude might first of all be characterized ... from the emotional point of view as a sur-*render* of the self to the intuitional content of things, as a movement of profound trust in the unshakableness of all that is simply and evidently 'given,' as a courageous letting-oneself-go in intuition and in the loving movement toward the world in its capacity for being intuited. This philosophy faces the world with the gesture of the outstretched open hand, with open-eyed gaze."

In energy terms, this beautifully describes to me the concept of rhythm. I think, one of the most beautiful lines I ever read:

> "... Paradise blooms around us here on earth, and we fail to see it only because we do not wish to do so ... "
> Vyacheslav Ivanov, *Dostoevski, Freedom and the Tragic Life.*

14
Exploring Inner Space

IN THIS CHAPTER I'D LIKE to touch on some random thoughts of my own and others to add flesh and substance to the structure I've described.
Energy: In his writings, Ernest Homes says:

> All that means anything is that while we live, *We Live,* and wherever we go from here we shall keep on living . . .[1]

In *Seth Speaks* is the comment:
What is needed is a basic trust in the nature of vitality . . .

We seem to accept the idea that, naturally, all of us are afraid of dying. I think the opposite is true—that most people are afraid of being totally alive. To be alive means taking risks, letting go of the familiar for the unexplored, constantly moving into unpredictable, uncharted territory. We seem to strive for security in the form of external stability and conformity, yet the very essence of life is change. We are constantly in a state of flux internally. Parts of us are dying while other parts are being born. The only real security lies in trusting that evolutionary flow to consistently lead us in the direction of growth, expansion, and joyous experience.

The spiritual healer, Ambrose Worrall, said:

> I believe there is a field of energy, akin to life itself, around and about us. There is an inexhaustible supply of energy around us. Our only problem is in tapping the source of supply.[2]

Such energy focuses like electricity. If we can handle it, it produces tremendous power; if we get overloaded, it will burn us out. The secret is in evolving into the awareness and use of such power so that we feel in charge of it and not overwhelmed by it.
Meditation as a route to expansion: From Edgar Cayce:

> For hours, or even days, after meditation had done its proper work, one would find that the answers he needed would occur to him—not in some strange, occult way, but in the heightening of the flow of ideas and impulses that had always been there.....Sometimes it would bring a heightening of sexual energies, or a quickening of other emotions and drives, which then needed to be faced and given constructive expression. For this process was calling forth the total life force in an individual.[3]

In the deepest recesses of the meditative experience, the mind is passive while the consciousness is awake and alert. When the head is turned off in this way, the intuitive self can operate freely, unblocked and flowing naturally. In that state the individual develops a sense of himself in his rhythmic, non-static form. He becomes an exquisitely sensitive instrument, attuned to the subtlest nuances of change and awareness within and around him.

Intuitive direction:

> In every realm of a man's life, from the most practical problem of starting a stalled car to the blinding problem of handling the sudden death of a loved one, he could count upon a quiet flow from within, trying to show him patterns, meanings, connections, directions, until he could say to himself in a click of recognition 'So that's how it is!'[4]

> In my opinion, you should be very careful about believing what someone else tells you. But you can be sure, very sure, of what you know from within to be true...[5]

I tell my students that the head and its logic can confuse you or lead you astray, but the intuition never errs. In the process of letting go and letting things come to you, one accepts hunches, fleeting thoughts, sharp flashes of perception, and with such acceptance comes increasing depth of awareness and understanding. Intuition is the ability to know apart from any reasoning process.

> The world society today is operating almost exclusively in an inaudible and non-visible area of the physical universe. I think it is safe to say that 90% of all the important work now being done by man relating to his evolutionary advance is work going on in the area above and below the tunable range of man's direct optical participation in the electro-magnetic spectrum.[6]

> There is hardly a writer even half-alive who hasn't said, 'It came to me. It was like taking dictation.'[7]

Unlimited power:

No limits, Jonathan? he thought, and he smiled. His race
to learn had begun.[8]

If you want to know what power is, and you want to store
it, you must tackle everything yourself.[9]

We are limited, not by Principle, but by our own inability
to see perfection.[10]

I find that many people shy away from a sense of personal power.
It is as though we perceive power as synonymous with loneliness.
Most of us do not know how to form relationships from a position
of power. We tend to develop relationships based on what we perceive
as need, dependency or weakness. Therefore, to accept that we are
totally in charge of ourselves, self-sufficient, and able to take care
of ourselves is the same as saying we want to be alone.

In addition, when an individual progresses along the pathway
of expanded consciousness, he does tend to lose some of his old connections. This happens without his having to do or say anything to
precipitate such loss. It is just that the distance between him and others
who do not move with him on the same journey becomes too great.
At the same time, he does not immediately attract new friends who
are on the same pathway because there is again that limbo period
in which he is saying goodbye to the old and preparing the way for
the next stage of his growth in his relationships. As he begins to do
what fits for him and to trust his intuitive direction, he experiences
himself in the process of moving away from some of his friends or
some of his friends moving away from him, a process that seems
out of his control. His only recourse is to trust, on faith, that his expanded levels of consciousness will not betray him no matter what
the current external reality appears to be. He has to trust that the
limbo period is necessary to his evolution as a space in which new
ways of being with other people can emerge for him that are based
on mutual enhancement of growth rather than need or lack.

Addictions:

As long as our personality systems are conditioned to react
to externals, according to stimulus-response principles of
conditioning instead of being able to respond to inner direction, fixed attitudes, feelings, and perceptions will continue

to crystallize at the different levels of consciousness, obstructing the free flow of energy.[11]

Creation of our own world:

The moment that a man becomes aware of his own soul and is endeavoring to control his own path in life, the influence of the planets, per se, definitely weakens and steadily becomes less and less...[12]

He then becomes more receptive to the forces flowing through the planets, rather than the forces of the planets, and to the subtler and higher energies of the solar system. The capability of biological life forms, especially man, to act as energy transformers is one of the key concepts of esoteric philosophy and is implicit in astrology.[13]

In my experience, I have used the I Ching, Tarot, astrology, and psychic readings as aids in deepening my awareness of myself and expanding my consciousness. However, I have reached the point where I have gone beyond those aids. I do not mean that in the sense that I am better than or smarter than the old masters who developed these worthwhile tools. It is just that I have reached a depth of awareness inside myself beyond which any external stimuli can probe. Again, that experience is first perceived as a lonely state. To realize that all of the answers, for you, are inside of you, is to give up the guru, the teachers, the parent forever. We are all truly alone in this sense. However, the acceptance of that reality makes it possible for us to achieve a sense of oneness with all around us that is not possible when the focus of our energy is on maintaining an external relationship or form at all costs.

No matter what may be in the subjective state of our thought, the conscious state can change it ... Man's conscious thought, acting through Law, may change any condition in his experience, provided he can clearly conceive of such conditions being changed ... Fear is the negative use of faith ... Don't vibrate to that which you do not wish to experience ... How much life can any man experience? As much as he can embody ... Intelligence is conscious energy working upon unformed substance in accord with law ... Everything our thought rests upon is either retarded or quickened by the power of that thought.[14]

It is impossible for us not to create. If we do not take conscious charge of what we are creating, we will become victims of our own lethargy, denial or negligence. Our lives will reflect the chaos of un-controlled energy which appears to confirm our acceptance of ourselves as helpless victims buffeted by a will-o-the-wisp, unfair, unreasonable fate. As long as an alcoholic says he drinks because of you or circumstances or because he just can't help it, he will con-tinue to drink to destruction. The minute he takes responsibility that he is making the choice to drink for some purpose that he does not yet understand, he will grow by that acceptance, regardless of whether he stops drinking or not. The acceptance of that responsibility halts the process of looking for answers outside of himself. The termina-tion of that search leaves a space for the intuitive levels of informa-tion to begin to emerge.

> It is not life that kills us but rather it is our reaction to it, and this reaction can be to a significant extent self-chosen.[15]

> The intensity of a feeling or thought or mental image is . . . the important element in determining its subsequent physical materialization . . . As long as you believe your en-vironment to be objective and independent of yourself, then to a large extent you feel powerless to change it . . . The thought unspoken is a 'sound' that you do not hear, but that is very audible at another level of reality and perception.[16]

Conservation of energy:

> You must learn to conserve energy and to control the emo-tional and mental expenditure and wastage that continually takes place in everyday life.[17]

Tremendous reserves of energy are required in order to repress what we feel, to control our environment and to drive ourselves to produce. While we may be utilizing these processes for learning, we need to be aware of the tremendous cost on an energy level. Our current energy crisis in national resources is a reflection of the inter-nal crisis we are experiencing in this area. It is time for a change. Even though we are afraid, we are ready to move into uncharted territory.

> Surrounded by energy and being an energy system, we are either attracting or repelling.[18]

We cannot be static or neutral. We are either attracting positive, enriching energy to us or negative influences which are draining us. We are either repelling negative energy so that it does not get fed and therefore dissipates, or we are attracting it and sustaining it be the force of our attraction.

> If one were doing the work he should be doing, he would not become tired . . . Really giving to others does not tire the giver.[19]

The energy around us is inexhaustible. If, in our work or play, we are not either pushing ourselves or resisting ourselves, we would feel high from whatever we are doing rather than exhausted. If our giving flows freely out of desire and not from duty or sacrifice, that experience also leaves us in a state of fullness rather than depletion.

> Energy which cannot express itself crystallizes and becomes inoperative.[20]

Evolution:

> To live only on the physical plane is to become a brute. To live on the intellectual plane alone might produce a learned and a scientific man, but he would lack true perception. To live only on the spiritual plane might cause one to become a dreamer without any practical way of making his dreams come true.[21]

> Stability has to do with the integration of pleasure, purpose, accomplishment, and identity . . . It takes study, development and experience before an identity can learn to hold its own stability in the face of such constant stimuli . . . Permanency of form is an illusion, since all consciousness must be in a state of change . . .[22]

I think that the key to evolution is balance. It seems to me that for the first time in our history we have the potential for moving into expanded levels of consciousness from a position of equilibrium. Our intellectual processes, our knowledge about and ability to assert feelings, and our awareness of and ability to trust intuitive processes have all begun to catch up and keep pace with each other. That position of balance makes it possible for us to speed up our evolution by gigantic leaps.

... The soul stands at the center of itself, exploring, extending its capacities in all directions at once.[23]

Rhythm:

The role of rhythm in man's well-being has not been demonstrated, but like the suspicion that a lack of rhythmicity spells illness, animal data make one suspect that well-being in man also depends upon a knowable harmony of internal rhythms coupled with a rhythm of overall behavior, synchronized in turn with the alteration of day and night—roughly every twenty-four hours.[24]

One of the most important things for parapsychology is our recent discovery of currents that flow in the body that are neither blood nor electrical.[25]

World evolution:

If a man's feet hurt, he hurts all over. And so it is with humanity. The downtrodden ones are the feet.[26]

'Life forces denied the light of day strengthened and soured in the night until the furies rode with the Valkyrie,' (according to Carl Jung in relation to Nazi Germany.) 'Germany hurtled into the eye of the irrational, dragging the rest of the world with her.' Cases of national mania would continue, Jung thought, until we work through to a better grasp of the unknown parts of our nature.[27]

Human society today is faced with the dilemma of a breakdown or breakthrough in human consciousness to match the breakthrough in science and technology.[28]

I believe, with Ernest Holmes, that the body—individually and collectively—is a concrete manifestation, existing in time and space, for the purpose of furnishing a vehicle through which life may express itself.

15

Examples Translating Theory into Practice

I HAVE BEEN USING THESE CONCEPTS in the therapy that I do as well as in my own life, and I want to share some examples to add to your understanding of this energy framework.

A family, consisting of both parents and three children—a girl eleven, a boy thirteen, and a boy fifteen, came to see me because the parents felt the fifteen-year-old was not utilizing his potential. He was a brilliant boy and just barely passing in school. He didn't seem to have any particular interests or projects except just to enjoy himself. His parents were frustrated and worried because they didn't want him to make mistakes that would cause him pain and difficulty later on. However, nothing they did seemed to motivate him.

I asked the parents what they might be learning by having a son who was so frustrating to them in this way. At first they thought that question didn't make any sense. When I persisted, they responded with negative information; "I'm learning I shouldn't have had children," and, "I'm not as good at parenting as I thought I would be." I pursued the question further and asked them what they were learning that was positive. As we explored, the father said that when he was his son's age, he could come home with a grade of 98, and his parents would ask him where the other two points were. He would then go back and make sure he got 100. He guessed he was still like that, and his son was just the opposite. He wondered if maybe his son was trying to save his life. The whole family began to talk at this point about how concerned they all were about husband and father because they felt he drove himself, didn't relax enough, and they were genuinely afraid he might have a heart attack at an early age. The daughter said that, while her brother carried it to the extreme because he was so totally opposite to the father in his behavior, maybe that was the only way her father would pay attention.

I then asked the fifteen-year-old son what he was learning by having parents who constantly pushed him to perform in ways that he did not want to adopt. He discovered that their pushing him was forcing him to really define himself around what he wanted rather than just to drift or conform to someone else's standards. Although it probably didn't show from the outside, he felt he was really struggling on the inside with a lot of questions about what he wanted in life. At present, he knew he didn't want to kill himself being a perfectionist like his Dad, but he didn't know what he did want either.

At this point, the whole family began to deal with how come they asserted from a duty, should, judgment framework and did not seem to make room for how they felt and what made them happy. Suddenly the fifteen-year-old was not the family's only problem. Everyone in the family was struggling with the same issue and reacting to it in different ways.

In another instance, I talked with a woman whose twelve-year-old son had been killed in an accident six months before. She had gone through the tears and anguish over his death and was now trying to put the pieces of her life back together again. I asked her what she had learned from her life experience with that particular boy. She said that he had been special in that he had been the one she leaned on after she and her husband had divorced five years ago. She had four children. He was not the oldest, but he had always seemed old far beyond his years. He had been the one to give her understanding, warmth, and support during that difficult period. I asked if she still needed that kind of assistance, and she said she didn't. She was now seeing another man whom she planned to marry. She had started school that fall and planned to get a master's degree. She had felt she was now at a place where she could give her son the kind of parenting and support she felt he had missed. I indicated that on an energy level they had given beautiful gifts to each other. He had lived to see her move from a state of despondency to independence and the beginning of fulfillment. She had recognized and appreciated his sensitivity and deep caring so that she was able to allow him to give to her in a special way. She could see beyond his childish form to the old soul inside. They each had grown by their experience with the other.

In my own deeper levels of consciousness, I felt, as I listened to her, that her son had come into this life primarily to assist her in her development. His mission was completed in that she no longer needed him in the same way, and he could then go on about his own business and focus on his own evolution. As I explore my own deepening levels of awareness, I feel more and more strongly that there are many levels on which we develop and that life evolves in other forms of consciousness, other planets, other worlds. I feel that many times there are children born to us whose souls are older, more mature than our own. How many times have you looked into the eyes of an infant or a small child and experienced a puzzling sense of recognition, an awareness that superceded the difference in body structure and age? I have wondered how different we would be with our children if we considered that, although they are in small bodies, their souls may be as much or more evolved than our own. Consider that each child is an entity in charge of his own journey and that he has chosen us just as we have chosen him—for purposes of learning and growing. It doesn't matter whether you believe that totally. Just considering that possibility will open up new depths of communication between you and your child on an energy level. I have even suggested to people who have made the decision to become parents but have not yet conceived, to try, in meditation, to carry on a conversation with the entity who is waiting to be born to them. Whether you believe such a thing is possible isn't important. What is important is that that kind of exploration will open up new dimensions of your own consciousness previously unavailable to you. Perhaps there is a part of each of us that knows what kind of person our child will be. In the process of carrying on an on-going conversation with that child (do this by playing both parts in a dialogue between you and your imagined child), you can understand in greater depth what having a child will mean to you and what your previously hidden hopes about this experience are. You can also begin the process of differentiating yourself and your child's personality so that he or she will not so easily be seen as an extension of you but as a totally separate person, right from the moment of conception.

I believe that in recent years we have taken responsibility for our children to the point that we have denied them personalities of their own. Certainly, children do reflect the personalities of their parents in many ways, and their behavior reflects the nature of the system in which the family operates. However, the child's behavior and his personality are a result of his own unique entity and natural rhythm also. Each individual in a family will handle life's events in entirely different ways. Each makes choices from the moment of birth—about eating, sleeping, touching, being held and cuddled—that are unique to his or her particular personality. Some infants are relaxed; others are determined. Some seem to dissolve in your arms while others give strong signals about being held or set apart. Each child is his own person from the beginning. Making contact with him, or about him (whichever way you prefer to see the process), with the more knowledgeable part of yourself who knows about him ahead of time, is a way of preparing the way for mutual respect, awareness, and communication between you and the personality who will join you in this concrete world at birth.

In another example about communication on an energy level, a young woman was telling me about a dream she had had recently in relation to her husband from whom she had been divorced for two years. She was upset about the dream because she thought she had let go of him; she had no desire to have any contact with him, and she saw the dream as an indication that she had not grown as much as she thought she had. In addition, she had received a letter from him two days after the dream, saying that he would be in her area and would like to see her. She had no desire to see him but was confused about the whole process.

I offered to her that we live with the assumption that dreams, fantasies, images, and messages that come to us from others on an intuitive level are products of our imaginations and not real. Suppose they are real and that a mutual process of communication is going on between us and others on other levels of consciousness? I acknowledged her stand that she did not want contact with her former husband on a concrete level. Their inability to connect satisfyingly on that level had brought about the divorce. However, perhaps there were aspects of their relationship that they were working out on another level of consciousness involving learning they could still get from each other. If she could explore her dreams and fantasies about him from that basis, then she could get every vestige of value from that experience without depreciating herself because she hadn't let go or was still hanging on to a destructive relationship.

For example, I thought it was important for her to know that she had not made a mistake in marrying him. Many of the qualities she thought were there when she married him *were* actually there. It was just that the concrete aspect of his development did not support those qualities. When she first met him, she sensed a lot of power and aggressiveness in him which she liked because she felt it fit with her personality. Those qualities were really there, but he was holding them back in order to develop the more passive parts of himself. So, she had given him a consistent message that she was disappointed in him. On the dream level, she kept seeing him as aggressive and expansive, and she was always running from him. When I asked her to look at that as real, she was shocked at first. Then she considered that something in her was blocking her from connecting with the kind of man she thought she wanted. Later, in therapy, she became aware that she was afraid of a man who was really in charge of himself and not overly dependent on her because she would lose control of the relationship. She was not trusting herself that someone could love her and be reliable for her if she didn't have a "hold" on him.

Many times we act out our most violent feelings on a dream level so that we have greater control of our conscious behavior. If we could appreciate that process instead of being afraid of it, we could utilize it with increasing effectiveness. We could experience it as a way to dissipate negativity safely and appreciate the life within us that produces intense feelings, whatever they are.

How many times have you thought or dreamed of someone you haven't seen for awhile, and suddenly that person writes or calls. My sense is that the concrete manifestation is simply a validation of the contact that has already been going on on another level of consciousness. The other person may not be able to acknowledge that such contact is occurring because he or she doesn't want to admit openly the depth of your connection with each other. So, he or she may admit only the obvious, rational explanation for the contact. However, many times I have called someone whom I had been "seeing" in my dreams or images to ask if there was a message for me and had that person respond, "Yes, I've been thinking about you often and have wanted to call." If you want to have some fun, begin to treat your dreams and images as real contacts and check out their reality in your important relationships.

In my work as a therapist, I have frequently heard people anguish over what they experience as the premature end of a relationship—either because of death or the decision of the other person. The widowed or rejected partner did not feel that he or she had the opportunity to finish, resolve, or complete the experience. He had many feelings left unsaid, felt misunderstood or unappreciated, or unseen by the other person. I believe that there are many instances in which we cannot relate to someone on a concrete level but can connect on other levels of consciousness where we are more evolved, more mature, less threatened or pained. Consider that dreams, fantasies, and images are actual mutual communication experiences. Then you can offer yourself the opportunity to explore many other avenues as a way of completing, resolving, and finishing experiences. With those resources open to us, we can totally let go with the inner assurance that we have achieved maximum learning from that experience. With that assurance, there is no sense of failure—only one of sadness that the concrete level of being could not match the intensity of evolution of the other levels of consciousness.

I recall a brief, very intense relationship I had with a man friend several years ago which he ended abruptly so that I felt cut off, without the opportunity to allow my feeling to run its natural course. He indicated his feeling for me had dissipated, but that was not my perception. I still felt the intensity of our connection but experienced him as denying that intensity because he was afraid of losing control—that if he loved too much, he would be swallowed up, overwhelmed, taken advantage of, or abandoned. I realized that I had allowed myself the relationship to learn how to keep owning my own feelings even though the other person wasn't responding as I wished. In the past, I would have sensed the change, cut off my own feelings, and gotten out first. However, that process cut into my own growth and was depreciating to me. It was important for me to respect my ability to love and honor my feelings without having to have someone else validate me in order for me to express the loving part of myself. Therefore, I felt the pain of being cut off in mid-stream was worth it, but I still felt unfinished. Several months ago, I had a dream, in which this man appeared to me. He expressed sadness at his loss, in that he had not been able to follow through all the way with a total commitment to his feelings. He said he was still not at that place in

his development. He felt he was moving and growing and was please
he was at the point where he could experience his loss withou
depreciating himself or trying to force his pace. When I woke up,
remembered the dream clearly, and I felt totally finished, with th
awareness that on some level of our consciousness we could pa
friends.

In another instance, I saw a woman in therapy who is an ac
complished artist. Her work was gaining increasing praise and recogni
tion, her family life was going reasonably well, and she felt she wa
growing personally in ways that were satisfying to her. However, she
found herself chain-smoking, drinking, and partying far too much
None of this interfered with her work or with her functioning in he
family. However, it made her uncomfortable because she thought such
behavior didn't really fit her, and she didn't seem to be able to cur
tail it. As I let myself sense her on an energy level, I experienced he
inner self as extremely delicate, not fragile, but delicate in the sense
of ability to perceive whispers instead of shouts, touches instead o
shoves, raindrops instead of tidal waves. I experienced her inne
rhythm as a soft flow, like a woodland stream gently lapping agains
the banks in a steady, almost imperceptible movement. I asked he
how that compared with her sense of herself. She was startled an
indicated she saw herself as hard-driving, hard-working, flamboyant
and even gross in her behavior at times. I suggested that, if she func
tioned that way, perhaps her over-imbibing of liquor and tobacco wa
an indication of the cost to her in going against her natural rhythm

When she began to consider this possibility, she realized tha
she had pushed and driven herself all of her life. As a child, she hac
survived a psychotic mother that way. As an adult, she had gainec
considerable recognition and success. To consider letting go of tha
drive and beginning to trust her inner direction and flow was a terri
fying thought, but perhaps she was at a point in her life where she
was ready to do that, even though it was frightening. The ability to
drive and push had been like a good friend whom she could lovingly
embrace and bid goodbye because they no longer fit and were go
ing in different directions. I asked her not to make any impulsive
decision—just consider that, because she felt her habits were con
trolling her rather than flowing from her, perhaps a part of her con
sciousness was giving her the message that she was interfering with

her rhythm in some important way. If she just gave herself the space to assimilate what I had offered, her insides would let her know what part was fitting and what was not and would give her the next step. What was important was for her to understand that her smoking and drinking compulsions were saying something important to her in terms of her current stage of growth and that as she understood the message and no longer needed those compulsions they would disappear. Later she indicated to me that she experienced those compulsions as brakes. She was moving very fast in the development of her intuitive processes and was becoming afraid that the development of her expanded consciousness would jeopardize her marriage and her work. As she realized that, she felt more in charge of her process and could appreciate that she was continuing to move and grow, and she was handling that growth in the best way she knew at that moment. That awareness alone, while it did not immediately resolve the problems, did begin to dissipate them. She saw them as part of her growth process and, therefore, temporary protective measures while she developed the sense of inner awareness and security to handle her power and expansiveness.

A couple came to see me because they were concerned that they had not yet conceived a child. There were no physical problems, and they wanted to explore whether or not there was something wrong emotionally that was getting in the way. I asked what they were learning by being in this situation in which they both wanted a child very much, yet no pregnancy was occurring. She indicated that she was becoming very depressed. She had quit her job six months before in the hope that being at home and not under pressure would help her get pregnant. However, nothing was happening, and she was getting bored and restless. This was the first time in her adult life that she didn't have many projects going all at once.

I asked her to describe her depressions, and she indicated that she felt a deep sense of loneliness, sadness, and isolation. I suggested she close her eyes and allow herself to feel those feelings without trying to analyze them, shut them off, or push herself—just sink into them. As she let herself do this, I asked if she had any images. She indicated that she saw herself as a small girl—four or five years old, and as she described herself as a child she began to cry. She then indicated that the first few years of her life her mother was ill and her father was working very hard, so she felt alone and frightened much of the time. She began to realize that much of her frantic activity was to cover those feelings of terror, which she still carried with her, and to keep them from coming to the surface. I told her that those feelings were like a weight inside of her, interfering with her ability to relax and get in touch with her natural rhythm. She could not allow herself to experience those feelings as a child because there was no one to go to with them, and they would have been overwhelming. However, now she was at a place in her life where her external nest was stable and solid, and it was time to allow herself to experience those feelings so that she could lay them to rest and go on with her life free of that burden. It was clear that, on a deep level of her consciousness, she wanted her child to emerge out of a free and flowing emotional state and not be another means by which she could occupy herself and escape her pain. The process of just experiencing the feeling would be a cleansing one, and she would be free to relate to her child with no barriers in the way.

Her husband indicated that her depressions and moping behavior were beginning to annoy him, and, because they were becoming prolonged, he was being forced to assert his annoyance. That was a new process for him because he had always been a "nice guy" who was continually understanding and forgiving no matter what he was feeling inside. He was beginning to realize now that when he did get mad at his wife the world did not come to an end and that he felt closer to her than he ever had before. His assumption of an attitude of agreeableness, when he did not really feel that way inside, was a way of protecting himself because he was not sure she would continue to care about him if he expressed who he really was.

As we worked together, both of them began to understand that they had a little more growing up to do before a baby would come along; that, in a more knowledgeable part of themselves, they wanted to be whole people who were in charge of themselves so that the baby could be an expression of their increasing intimacy and not a substitute for it.

In still another therapy situation, a man came to see me who had just separated from the woman he had been seeing for two years. He was feeling obsessed about her—dreaming of her, having anxiety attacks around the possibility that she was seeing someone else driving by her house to check up on her. When we explored what his obsession was contributing to his growth, he recognized that he was attaching his sense of security and worth to a person other than himself. He was handing over part of his power to someone else by accepting her behavior as a judgment about himself and by functioning as though he could not survive without her. He began to realize that that was the way in which he grounded himself. He had been a loner in growing up, with a highly developed fantasy world. It had been easier for him, in many ways, to withdraw from life and other people. So, he felt he was investing others with power over him to force himself to come out of his shell and learn how to involve himself with others. He realized that what he was doing was not the best way for him, but it was the only way he knew at present. In the midst of all the pain, he was feeling more alive and getting a stronger sense of what fit for him as a way of relating. it was as though he had to wallow in his symptom (his need to give others the power to validate and judge him as a way of connecting with them) so that he could experience it on every level of his consciousness. Via the process of such a total experience he could know on the deepest levels of himself what that way of functioning cost him and what it did for him. Until he knew on all those levels that that process was costing more than it was doing for him, he was not prepared to give it up.

It has often been my experience that an individual may make a decision that a certain way of functioning does not fit for him, and he wants to give it up. However, he may temporarily intensify that behavior as a way of experiencing, as well as knowing, that it does not fit for him any longer. For example, I knew a homosexual man who used to frequent certain bars as a way of picking up other men. He suffered a number of humiliating experiences with men he met in this way who manipulated him and used him in depreciating ways. He was very upset by his inability to cease doing this in the light of such experiences. I indicated to him that he would probably continue that practice until he learned, experientially, that there were worse things for him than being alone. When he really understood that in the deepest levels of his consciousness, then he could be in charge of his behavior in a way that was more fitting to who he was.

A young couple came to see me who were both talented, bright, and extremely articulate. They were experiencing great distance and pain in their relationship. I asked them to begin to talk to each other about their concerns and allow me to watch their interaction so that I could see what was going on. As they did this, it was evident that their manner of communicating consisted of blaming and judging each other, and defending and explaining themselves. It looked as though they were in a courtroom presenting their respective cases with all the supporting evidence clearly documented. They were both probably right in their various grievances, but the whole process merely succeeded in keeping them at arm's length from each other. They could have tape recorded their arguments and gotten as much satisfaction out of just flipping on the tape recorder. There was no more actual contact than that as they talked at each other. I shared that observation with them and wondered what that process was doing for them. They both admitted that it was keeping them very distant from each other. I asked what that distance was doing for them in a positive way. As we worked on that idea, they discovered that the distance was very necessary at this period of their individual growth. In the beginning of their relationship, they had functioned as though they were one person—doing everything together, never apart. That period of their connection had given them enough sense of security that they had begun to risk branching out and risking parts of themselves they had never risked before. He had left a very secure job that he hated and was trying a totally different field of work. He didn't know as yet if he wanted to stay in it, but she felt he was learning about himself in some important ways as a result of the experience. She had developed one of her hobbies to the point that it was beginning to pay financially, and that had bolstered her self-esteem considerably. They had begun to make friendships with more people who were not exactly like themselves and, as a result, were beginning to question some of their values which they had always thought were inviolate.

Now each was at a place to break the old dependent connection they had had with each other so that they could experiment even more with their individuality. As they realized this, they began to take distance from each other without having to hurt themselves to do so and without seeing the distancing as a betrayal of their commitment to each other or a statement that something was drastically wrong with the marriage.

A young woman came to see me who had been having an affair with a married man for two years. She had been living with the hope that he would divorce his wife and marry her but was beginning to realize that that was and probably always had been the furthest thing from his mind. She could not understand why she had allowed herself to get into such a situation and why she was having trouble getting out of it even when she was convinced she was being used.

As we explored her predicament from a positive framework of growth, she discovered that she had been a professional victim. She was always getting herself into situations in which she ended up being manipulated, being a martyr, or experiencing intense, uncontrollable rage at being mistreated or unappreciated. When we talked about what that victim framework was doing for her, she realized that she was very frightened of her own power. She was afraid that if she really trusted her feelings and her intuitive processes, they would take her into risky, unstable, unpredictable territory. Being a victim was a way of keeping herself grounded, tying up her energy, and connecting with other people. She usually had gruesome stories to tell. People were always feeling sorry for her. And her presentation of herself as a helpless victim kept people from being threatened by her very real power.

As she got in touch with that reality, she recognized that she was ready to give up that process. She felt strong enough now to risk being alone. However, she felt she wasn't ready to give up her victim role suddenly and totally. She would have to do it gradually, in balance with her ability to understand, appreciate and utilize her intuitive process so that she would feel in charge of them and not be swept off her feet.

I saw a family recently who had multiple symptomatology. The mother was depressed and had been hospitalized several times for short periods during the last two years. The oldest daughter had run away several times and had also been in juvenile hall because of drug usage. The middle child was a non-achiever in school and suffered numerous somatic complaints. The youngest child had uncontrollable temper tantrums, and the father was a periodic alcoholic. The family was referred by the wife's physician for treatment. When I saw them, each person in the family whined about how helpless he or she was, what an impossible situation all were in, and had multiple evidence to prove there was no way out. The wife said that if she came out with her feelings, her husband started drinking or would leave her. If she didn't, she got depressed and had to be hospitalized. The husband felt that if he complained to his wife, she got unreasonably angry, so he just kept to himself. The children all felt that no matter what they did it didn't make anyone happy or pleased.

As I sat with the family, I heard all their complaints and all their protestations of weakness. However, in my gut I experienced tremendous energy held down at tremendous cost. I shared that perception with the family and asked them what they felt would happen if they were powerful instead of weak and helpless. Beginning with the mother, I had each of them draw a picture of the way he or she saw the family functioning now and the way the family would be if he or she were strong and powerful. The mother's first picture showed her in a partially stooped position, leaning on two of the children for support and at the same time trying to hold them up. She saw the father and the oldest daughter turned away from her. When I asked how she felt looking at that picture, she said it was impossibly uncomfortable; she couldn't keep that position much longer.

In her second picture, she saw all the family members leaving her, and she was standing alone. I asked her to allow herself to experience that alone place and to feel what it cost her and what it did for her. She felt relief, but she also felt fear rising in her throat like a scream. I indicated to her that she did not have to make a choice. Neither place was bad or good. It was a matter of determining what fit for her and each of the family in their current growth process. What was important was for each to recognize he or she did have a choice. Then each could let himself feel his way back and forth between those choices. Each person's insides would make the decision. No one had to force himself in any way. He just had to take responsibility for his choice and allow himself room to go whatever way fit for him without depreciating or judging himself, but with respect for whatever that choice was doing for him in the current moment.

16
More Examples

IN MY CLASSES, many people have shared examples with me about how these energy concepts have influenced their lives.

One man indicated to me that he found himself quite frightened and often feeling "spaced out" at the end of a class session. He began to realize that he was functioning with a rigid control structure based on a judgmental framework. He was afraid of his intuitive processes because he thought his feelings were unreliable and would take him into unfamiliar, reckless territory. However, he also realized that his judgmental framework was not working for him anymore because it was too constricting. He began to experience a kind of war going on inside of him between his logical, reasonable side and the intuitive, feeling side of himself. Several weeks after the course was ended, he suffered a slipped disc in his back. He was in traction for three weeks, and during that time he experienced pain and emotional upset. However, he was surprised to find himself also feeling a sense of joy and great relief. As he explored all of these feelings, he realized that he was letting go of attempting to control his external environment in favor of trusting his intuitive processes to direct and take care of him. He saw his physical problem as an external manifestation of that internal shift—the crumbling of his control structure.

A woman, who was also in one of my classes, had had difficulty with eruptions in her mouth and throat and was informed by her doctor that she might have cancer. She was very frightened and upset at that possibility; however, she found herself looking at it from the viewpoint we had discussed in the course—what was the experience saying to her in terms of her growth? All of her life she had been plagued by various illnesses and trauma. She began to consider that she did not have to live her life defined around suffering. The suffering she had already experienced had developed an emotional depth and sensitivity in her, but she realized she was hanging on to suffering beyond its usefulness to her because it was a familiar way to live. Suffering had been her way of knowing she was alive—it provided a kind of drama and excitement in her life and brought her sympathy and concern from others. She recognized that she was clinging to her old patterns because she was afraid to take the risk to find excitement and aliveness in trying new things and developing parts of herself which made her feel unsure and a little frightened. However, she could see that this current illness was telling her that she could not continue to cling to her old way of life because it would kill her. As it turned out, she did not have cancer, but she did use the experience to let go of being sick and helpless and began to take risks in exploring what made her feel alive and creative.

Another woman indicated that she had always been very judgmental about everyone, including herself, and had never liked that quality in herself. During the course, she began to appreciate that her judgmental stance was a way of grounding herself. She noticed that every time she felt a little insecure, off-balance, or frightened, she would become critical of herself or others, and she would immediately feel comfortable and in control again. She had grown up in a judgmental family so, although she experienced that framework as restrictive and unpleasant, it was familiar and served to keep her and others in line. She recognized that she was afraid of new and unpredictable situations and that she would have to move gradually into trusting her feelings and her intuitive processes. Thus, each time she found herself falling into her judgmental position, she no longer chastised herself. Instead, she realized that was an indication she was moving too fast and needed to allow herself time and space to savor, digest, and assimilate each new experience into her changing picture of herself.

In another instance, a friend of mine related an experience to me in which she used a positive framework as a way of assessing her feelings and determining her actions. A friend of hers was experiencing financial difficulty because, in addition to having gone back to school and supporting two children, she had had some unexpected expenses arise which upset her budget plans. My friend thought of lending her money to survive until she could get back on her feet but, for some reason, held back on the offer. She indicated that in the past she would have felt selfish and ungiving, but this time she trusted that there was some other reason for her not wanting to give that she just didn't understand yet, so she respected her own feelings and did not make the offer. Later, she learned that a man with whom the woman had been deeply involved owed her three thousand dollars. She had not previously asserted enough pressure to get the money, but, with her financial predicament, she was forced to do so. She indicated to my friend that she was glad the situation had occurred because it had forced her to learn how to assert and take a stand for herself in a new way. My friend then realized that if she had offered her a loan she would have interfered with her evolutionary journey and that, on a deeper level, some part of her had known that all along.

A woman I know, for as long as she can remember, has had a phobia about riding in airplanes. She had always felt ashamed and annoyed because she could not seem to conquer it. As she shifted in her thinking to begin to consider what it meant in terms of her growth, she realized that it was an indication that she was having difficulty letting go of her controls enough to trust herself and her evolutionary journey. When she recognized that, she decided to go into therapy to understand what losing control meant to her and to develop a clearer sense of her own identity. She felt that the energy she had put into repressing her impulses had resulted in her feeling trapped and unhappy. Such repression had also masked her real identity, even to herself, because she had always forced herself to conform to some image that didn't fit her at all.

Another young woman, an acquaintance, had come to California from New York two years before. She had utilized her time here to focus intensively on growth in almost every facet of her life. She had developed a beginning reputation as an expert free-lance photographer, she had gone into therapy to develop her self-esteem and overcome her tendency to withdraw from life into periods of extreme depression, and she had developed several friendships which were nourishing and supportive to her. She decided suddenly to return to New York for Christmas to see a man friend with whom she had previously been intimately involved. She felt their relationship had ended abruptly when she left New York the first time and had remained incomplete and unresolved for her. Logically, the decision looked like a masochistic one. She was returning to a place that would be cold and lonely for her to see a man who had been lukewarm in his response to her proposed visit. However, she was determined to go, and the determination seemed to come from some reservoir deep inside of her against all logic or reason. Therefore, both her therapist and I supported her decision, indicating to her that the experience might be difficult, but it was obviously going to be vital in terms of her growth. As it turned out, she used the journey to trigger depths of despair and loneliness which she had always lived with but never let herself feel before. She had always been protected and treated as helpless by a family who had provided the necessities and even the luxuries of life but had also been cold and distant emotionally. On this trip, she faced all of her feelings connected with her childhood without running away or flinching and ended up feeling purged and strengthened. She had survived her worst fears. All of her ghosts were out in the open and didn't do her in. If she could survive that, nothing could ever daunt her again! In addition, she confronted her friend with all the unspoken anger and sadness which had previously been unexpressed, so that she felt free of him and pleased with herself for her ability to be honest and open in the face of his rejection. When she returned, her therapist thought she had probably saved herself nine months of therapy by that experience. She had obviously been ready to test herself in her own personal fire and on some level of her consciousness made the decision that was most vital to her growth, even though it looked foolhardy on the surface.

A woman came to see a therapist friend of mine, complaining that she kept developing lumps and cysts in various parts of her body—they seemed to come and go, and doctors could find no apparent cause. The therapist, who was experienced in looking at symptomatology in terms of positive growth processes, asked her if she had grown up in a family in which feelings were hidden. In exploring this possibility, the woman came to realize that the open expression of feeling and of information was blocked in her family and there were many "secrets" which everyone knew but no one talked about. Her father had had an affair which she had found out about through a neighbor. There had been financial difficulty which she had learned about by listening in on a phone call. Her mother had been seriously ill and gone to the hospital without anyone ever discussing the situation with her. Her grandfather died, and she never knew what was wrong with him, nor did she get to go to the funeral. It was as though he just disappeared off the face of the earth with no explanation and just barely a mention. She supposed that they had wanted to protect her, but the effect on her was to give her the message that she should keep her questions, fears, and anxieties to herself. She recognized that her body was now telling her it was time for everything to come out into the open—the process of keeping her feelings to herself was now hurting her, and she and her current family were ready to face everything squarely and openly. That awareness was the beginning of a major change for her as well as for her husband and children. The whole family entered into therapy. At first, the sessions consisted mostly of the expression of hidden fears, anger, hurt and guilt; but gradually a new aliveness and closeness began to take shape, and within six months her growths disappeared as "mysteriously" as they had come.

It has been my experience that when an individual makes a shift emotionally in terms of the way in which he defines himself, that shift is often accompanied by a physical expression. The physical manifestation may vary widely in degree of severity from a bad cold to a serious back ailment. He may have learned to function and express himself according to an internal structure based on right or wrong, good and bad, to which he adhered regardless of what he was really feeling inside. He had learned in his growing-up experience that such a structure earned him approval and kept him from getting criticized or ostracized in his family. However, as he continues to grow emotionally, he begins to shift in the direction of functioning according to what fits for him—what he likes and doesn't like—and to make his own rules based on that framework rather than someone else's judgments. The process of shifting from one framework to another is usually a gradual one. When he lets go of his last hold on the old structure, the energy cost is phenomenal. Such a total shift takes every last ounce of reserve. So the physical expression is an external validation of the total letting go that is occurring internally as well as a result of the energy cost of his extensive change. On the inside such a change feels like a death because the individual connects his whole identity to the structure around which he has defined himself. When it goes, it feels as though he is actually dying because he doesn't know who he is separate from that structure. Therefore, he must go into a limbo in which he feels awkward, young, and off balance. From that position, he begins to assert himself out of whatever feelings emerge and to build a new internal structure based on what fits him. That structure gives him a sense of identity and solidarity inside but is also flexible so it can be modified and developed according to his evolving identity and expansion of consciousness. Thus, he is not plagued by the paradox of attaching his sense of stability to something that also becomes his prison.

Anytime one attaches his sense of survival, stability, or security to someone or something outside of himself, he automatically puts a limit on his growth. He cannot follow any feelings that he thinks might jeopardize his position with the person, place, or thing which is his reason for living. If he has entrusted his survival, security, and happiness to his own identity and the intuitive processes within himself, he can go wherever his feelings and energy take him. There is no fear of loss or harm because he has faith in his own aliveness and his connection with the flow of life and energy around him.

I feel that our bodies constantly talk to us. If we would look at the body as a sensitive instrument, we would pay attention to its slightest nuance as a clue about potential growth direction. More often we tend to function as though the body is prone to accidents, illness, and forms of expression that have nothing to do with its owner's identity. There is no separation between body and psyche—they are inextricably bound together in a constant rhythmic flow. The slightest deviation from perfect health provides valuable data to explore in terms of an individual's overall growth process. It may be an indication that he is blocking the expression of some important feeling. He may allow himself to go along with someone else's wishes, thinking that what he wants isn't really all that important and he can go either way. However, if he finds himself consistently getting ill in such a circumstance, he may need to consider that he apparently feels more strongly about that decision than his logical mind perceives. This is often true of people who think of themselves as easy-going. Some people really are easy-going, but others have adopted that way of functioning because it appears to be less of a strain and keeps the boat from rocking. However, their bodies may be telling them that that way of functioning does not fit them. In fact, it is producing a wear and tear that is potentially much more dangerous than rocking the boat!

The body particularly talks to us in sexual situations. We get so absorbed by performance that we interpret body messages as indications of sickness, inadequacy, lack of caring, or age. If a woman tenses so that the insertion of a man's penis into her vagina is difficult or impossible, that body behavior is saying something about the relationship between her and her partner. If a man loses his erection or is impotent with his partner, again that body behavior is making a comment about that particular relationship. No matter that he has had the same experience with other women. The message may be entirely different with each partner, but there is a message. Expressions such as these are never isolated from the current relationship in process. The body may be saying that they do not fit with each other at all or do not fit at that particular time. It may be saying that there are some very important feelings that need to be communicated which they are holding back from each other. Or it may be saying that they are trying to make love when they really should be fighting or crying or expressing fear because that is what they are really feeling inside. Many people use sex as a cover for what they are feeling that they are afraid to express. Instead of the sexual feeling flowing from a deep reservoir of caring and desire for intimacy, it is really a defense against feeling afraid, insecure, alone or angry.

In even more subtle forms of expression, we often feel exhausted for no apparent reason, and we respond to that state by pushing ourselves even harder, feeling guilty because we're not working hard enough and don't have a reason for our slothfulness, or by depreciating ourselves for not performing as we should. If, instead, we respected our bodies and ourselves enough to consider that something must be going on on a level of our consciousness not immediately evident to us, we could utilize that clue to explore and learn more about our insides. That kind of appreciation tends to open up our deeper channels of knowledge about ourselves. We might find that we are letting go of something or someone inside and are utilizing a lot of energy handling the loss. Perhaps we are moving into a new situation or experience which is fraught with more anxiety and concern than we previously realized. Or perhaps someone around us is more of an emotional drain than is evident on the surface, and the body is sending messages to clue us in and encourage us to protect ourselves.

The point is to listen to the language of your body with respect, appreciation, and understanding. You may talk yourself into believing many things, but the body is never fooled. It always rebels against an attempt to force it into a mold. It has information immediately available to it that our minds do not always perceive. How many times have you gone to a meeting, a party, or just visiting some friends when everything looked fine on the surface, but all of a sudden you felt sluggish or out of sorts? If you said, "What am I picking up that doesn't fit for me?" instead of, "What's wrong with me?" you might be surprised at what you would learn. You would also begin to develop a respect and even awe at the wide range and delicacy of your perceptive mechanisms.

17
How to Interpret External Events

IF WE CONSIDER THAT EACH OF US is an energy system connected to all the universal energy around us, then we might also consider that external events in which we are involved are also saying something to us about the direction of our lives. We do not have to automatically believe or accept that premise. All we have to do is open our minds to that question, and the answer will come to us through a friend, through something we may read, or from the depth of our intuitive awareness. The secret is to explore that event from the standpoint of positive growth direction. So often when something happens that is unpleasant, frightening, or devastating in its impact on us, we make conclusions that we are cursed, unlucky, being punished, or we just give up. Our energy focuses on the negative aspects of the disaster and stays there, drawing us deeper into the maw. We then build a case that life is cruel, relentless in its unpredictability, and we are helpless pawns dependent on pure chance. How often have you said or heard the words, "Things are going so good, I feel uneasy—something bad is bound to happen." We are conditioned to that idea, not just in words, but in the deepest levels of our consciousness. Look at our superstitions (knock on wood, et cetera) which have been around so long their origins probably cannot even be traced. What do you have to lose by considering that your thoughts and emotional energy do have power and that, by shifting the focus of that power, you can change your world to suit your specifications?

For example, a friend of mine saw a piece of property that was her dream home and was determined to buy it even though it was far beyond her financial means. She tried every way she could think of to try to finance that property. Finally, she decided to invite other friends in on the investment since it was so huge a place it could be divided into separate apartments which others could live in or use as rental investment. Several people were interested, and she asked them to contact her real estate agent who had agreed to work out the financial arrangements for such a conglomerate. As it turned out, not one of them followed through. She then realized that every avenue had been cut off, and she was puzzled since that didn't seem to fit with the fact that she had originally found the place accidentally, it was exactly as she had always dreamed her home would be, and she had developed an instant liking for the woman who was the owner of the place. Their connection was so strong that the woman was willing to go out of her way to help make the place available. When my friend stopped pushing and began to look inside of herself for the answers to these seemingly contradictory facts, she felt that this home had appeared to her like a vision foretelling for her where she was going in her life. However, it was important not to tie herself down to a large place or big financial investment at this time in her life because she had many places to go and other parts of herself to develop. She felt that the process of events was saying to her, "Be patient, you can have it all—everything you are doing now is making it possible for you to be able to have every dream and to handle your success wisely." She recognized that one of her difficulties was her impulsiveness and impatience, qualities about herself she often enjoyed. However, at times they controlled her rather than her being in charge of them. She felt that the timing of events was forcing her to learn to trust her intuitive processes to do the best for her even though she couldn't see the result immediately.

She later bought another place that was smaller, required no upkeep, and yet was new and beautiful. She sees it as symbolic in terms of another positive step in her life, and that part of her growth is to learn how to enjoy and savor each step as a way of expanding her awareness and preparing the way for the next step.

In my own experience, I assert in the direction of getting something I want, but if my assertions get blocked, I stop and take stock. Perhaps I am going the wrong way for me, perhaps the timing is off and I need to wait awhile, or there may be another way of accomplishing the same thing that will emerge as better and easier for me. If I am in a situation in which there seems no avenue open to me, I let go and trust my intuitive processes to give me the answer when I need it. Again, my timing may be off. Other events that I do not know about may be developing and will change my course of action. It may be important for someone else to do what I am trying to do. Or there may be something I need to learn by staying in an unmobilized state.

All of my life I have heard from all directions that anything worth having required suffering, pushing ourselves past our limits, back-breaking work. If it comes easily, don't trust it. I now believe that just the opposite is true. If it doesn't come easily, I am interfering with my natural rhythm and deliberately piling up barriers in my pathway. Just as sonar seeks out a safe and smooth pathway for a submarine deep under water, so our intuitive processes, if we trust them, make our pathways smooth and trouble-free. Then our excitement and aliveness is generated by the expansion of our awareness and the constant discovery of new territory rather than by the hurdling of barriers and the conquest of obstacles.

Another example occurred as I have been writing this book. I did the first fifty pages and was in a hurry to send them to my publisher to get his reaction before I proceeded. I called the typist who had done my last manuscript and couldn't reach her. Then I called three others, and everyone was either out of town or busy. I started to panic, and then I relaxed and said to myself, "Okay, you're doing this the hard way. That belongs to the past. If you did it the easy way, you would look for a typist who lives close to your home and has enough time available to produce rapidly. Who do you know in this neighborhood who might know about a typist?" I thought of a man who had access to many business people in the community and called him. He answered on the first ring, and, in response to my request, he said that his wife was an expert typist and had just mentioned to him that morning that she wished she could find a way to make some extra money. Needless to say, I rushed the manuscript over to her, and she finished those first few pages beautifully and in record time. I have since learned that the book, as she has been typing it, has been extremely important to her in her own growth and development. It is as though everything fit to bring the best to all concerned. That is the magic and beauty of the energy process. All is in synchronism for the purpose of joy and growth.

Even in the most minor occurrence the flow is evident. A friend of mine had received a call from someone she had not seen in some time. He was coming to the area on business and wanted to take her to dinner, and he asked her to get a date for his partner whom he was bringing with him. She tried several people with no success and decided she wasn't going to push further. Maybe it was important for her to go out alone with both men for some reason. At the last minute, he called and cancelled the date because of an important business matter that had come up in the East. He came to her area again the following week, and she got a friend to go along with no difficulty at all.

Two women I know (I'll call them Jane and Susan) had once had a close friendship and then drifted apart because one began a growth spurt which put her into a new dimension. Much of their past connection had been built around mutual pain, struggle and depression. They could talk for hours about their problems and difficulties. Jane began to shift her focus consciously, and her life expanded accordingly, so they no longer had much to talk about. Suddenly, Jane realized that six months had gone by, and they hadn't even talked on the telephone. She had been so busy with the increasing success in her work and her love life that the time had slipped by. Just about this time, Susan called her and told her that at first she had been hurt and upset when Jane had not contacted her. Then she had begun to take stock of herself and realized she had depended on Jane and really didn't have many others friends, certainly none as close as Jane had been. As she thought of that, she also recognized that she wasn't that great to be around, and the only people who were drawn to her were the "losers." From that point on, she had begun to shift in terms of asserting how she wanted her life and herself to be and to take responsibility for bringing those desires about. Now she was calling to let Jane know what she had discovered about herself and that she was surprised and pleased about what she had accomplished so far. They talked for some time on the phone, and Jane said that she had pulled away because she had felt guilty about sharing her increasing success with Susan who seemed so depressed and unhappy. She realized as she talked that that was a depreciating stance and that the real reason was that she had felt so unsure of her new way of being that she would have let Susan's pain drag her down. So, she had pulled away to protect her new structure until she felt more sure of herself in that identity. They were both pleased about making contact again from a whole new way of relating, and they made plans to go skiing for the weekend.

Two days before Jane and Susan were to leave, Susan called to say she had fallen down the stairs and sprained her leg, so the trip was off. Jane thought about this and later called Susan back to inquire if her accident had anything to do with the process between them. She knew that Susan wanted to be friends again and she did, also. However, she knew that she (Jane) was at a very high, intense energy level at this time, and she wondered if that interfered with Susan's process at all. Susan heaved a sigh of relief and said that she had been wondering what was wrong with her because a part of her wanted to see Jane and a part of her didn't. Now, she recognized that she needed to move more slowly into the new relationship. The intensity of Jane's energy level was overwhelming to her, and she found herself losing contact with her own insides as she talked to Jane. She felt that what she needed was to see her, then have time to assimilate and integrate the experience so that she could use it to facilitate her own growth and not impede it. She got so carried away with Jane's enthusiasm that she could not discern what her own real feeling was. She felt she needed to touch base with Jane and then take space until her own new sense of herself was strong enough to handle the intensity they generated together.

Another friend (Elaine) and a man with whom she was having a very intense affair (Steve) had decided to go to Carmel for a weekend. They had a marvelous time—good food, gorgeous scenery, great sex and a tender, soft, loving time. Toward the end of their three day weekend, they were walking in the woods and saw a small deer who had just been injured and died in their arms. At first the incident cast a pall over their otherwise delightful weekend. Then they began to ask themselves what that event might mean in terms of their growth. Each of them came to the same awareness at almost the same time. They had originally met just as he was leaving a marriage and she was leaving a painful love affair. Their relationship had an intensely healing effect on each of them. They had shared their pain with great understanding and compassion and had been deeply appreciative of each other at the time when each had needed such appreciation the most. With their relationship to bolster them, they had begun life anew and were now experiencing the most expansive periods of growth either of them had ever known. Suddenly they saw the death of a small animal who had been suffering and died as a symbol of the death of suffering in both of their lives. Thus, the weekend was the end of an old way of being and the beginning of new life based on beauty, sensuality, and spirituality, all in perfect equilibrium.

Sometime later, they both experienced that they were distancing somewhat from each other and were puzzled by this. She was talking to me about their relationship one day when a bird flew into the sliding glass door of her living room and fell to the ground. She later mentioned this to Steve, and his first spontaneous, intuitive response was, "Look for hidden obstacles." When they considered that, both of them realized that their relationship had reached such a level of intensity that it fit for them either to get married or take space from each other. Neither felt that he or she was ready for marriage. He was not divorced, and her emotional process of letting go of her former relationship was not totally completed. They both felt that they had learned much from each other and that their relationship gave great impetus to their mutual growth. However, before they could go ahead with each other, they needed room to tie up all the loose threads that belonged to the past so that they could come together again out of joy and expansiveness rather than pain and loss. They wanted to be able to commit fully and freely with nothing in the way.

Again, I am not telling you by all of this to deny the reality of anything negative that happens to you. Face your pain, cry your tears, rage at circumstances or people—whatever clears your consciousness and spends all your feeling. However, at that point consider that something inside of you is always pulling you in a positive direction no matter what the current external reality appears to be. Once it has happened and you feel washed and relieved of feeling, let it go. It belongs to your past. Connect to your future in terms of growth and expansion as your permanent reality. When you are ready, look for positive direction in every experience. That pathway will lead automatically to the fulfillment of your most precious dreams, with the concurrent distillation of negative programming on every level of your consciousness.

18
Coincidences and Dreams

WHEN PEOPLE OR INCIDENTS OCCUR in our lives in unusually connected ways, we usually consider such occurrences as accidental events which we label as coincidences. I believe that such coincidences are really unique opportunities for growth spurts. It is as though an individual's energy system draws to him a set of circumstances which piques his curiousity, interest, or strong feeling to give impetus to his growth.

For example, a client of mine was very much in love with a man and had lived with him for two years when he decided to leave her. She felt shattered because she had committed herself very deeply to the relationship, and she had great difficulty letting go. After their initial split, when they moved into separate residences, they continued to see each other periodically. Her hope was that they could work things out, and he gave her some encouragement for that hope although he did not make any promises. After things dragged on for several more months in this unclear situation, she decided to take a trip to give each of them time to be alone and see how each really felt about the other. Another friend took her to the airport, and on the way she spotted her man in a car going in the opposite direction with a woman sitting beside him, apparently on a date. Now, for him to be on that road, which was fifty miles from where he lived, at that particular time was clearly unusual. That sight triggered her into the depths of her pain and loss. She felt betrayed that he would be out with someone else on the night he knew she was leaving, and she had a graphic picture that his commitment and feeling for her was not equal to what she felt for him. During her time away, she allowed herself to experience her loss totally for the first time, and when she returned she was ready to let go. She later said that if that incident had not occurred as it did, it would have taken her another three to six months to let go. As it turned out, she made remarkable strides in her growth the following year, and she realized that she really could not have afforded that extra few months. She needed to let go so that she could get on with her life. She had too much to do and too far to go to spend any more time in that unfruitful place.

Coincidences involve perfect timing and the prospect of being confronted with something important to one's growth. We can utilize them to great advantage if we keep open to their possible messages. Several years ago, I bought a brand new house, a place I thoroughly liked and enjoyed. After I had lived there for two years little things began to go wrong—nothing expensive or extreme, just annoying inconveniences. For example, the hot water heater broke down. I called someone who repaired heaters who came out to look at it but said I needed an electrician first. A small part was malfunctioning, but its repair required service from both the heater man and the electrician. After the electrician had done his job, the other man came back and did something which upset the electrician's work. As a result, we had to go through the whole routine all over. In addition to the expense, there was the difficulty of having to be away from my office to let the repairmen in the house and see what they were doing so I would know what to look for if the heater failed again. The whole experience turned out to be a tremendous hassle for so small a difficulty. At first I didn't pay any attention, but as this experience dragged on to become ludicrous, I began to get the feeling that it was time to sell my house. As I considered that possibility, the feeling became stronger and stronger. I didn't push anything but allowed myself just to consider how I felt about such a move. I found myself beginning to make a few changes that would improve the value of the house and slowly getting it in top condition. In addition, I was weighing the reality that, while I loved the place, it was a lot of responsibility, and I felt somewhat tied down by it. In addition, I would be doing more traveling in my work, and I would worry about leaving the house uninhabited.

I finally decided that I would offer the house for sale at a fixed, non-negotiable price and see what happened. One hour after I put the house on the market, my real estate agent sold it, at my price, to the first person who looked at it—a woman who had just moved from another state and loved the house at first sight. In addition, she liked and wanted all the furniture that I could not take with me to an apartment—the refrigerator, washer-dryer, and a kitchen set I could not use. Six months later I decided to reduce my time schedule in order to write my first book, and the money from the house was a vital back-up to allow me to do that without undue stress about finances. Also, someone began to build another house down the hill from mine which partially blocked my view. It did not decrease the value of my house since it was in prime territory, but it did decrease its value considerably for me, and I would have been very unhappy about that occurrence if I had still been living there.

I mentioned in an earlier chapter about the period in my business life in which my partner and I were expanding our activities to the point that we were both overwhelmed. At that point, we decided that we should hire someone to take over some of the administrative and organizational aspects of the business, but were were nonplused about how to find such a person. He or she would need to have ad-ministrative experience and be able to work part-time, since we could not afford a full-time person. At exactly that time, an old friend of mine called whom I had not seen in several years. He was a jack-of-all trades and master of many. He was in the process of shifting his field of interest, and he was looking for a part-time job. As he, my partner, and I talked together, it became clear he was perfect for us, and we offered something different enough from his past experience to interest him and offer him a growth opportunity. As it turned out, he literally saved our lives by taking the pressure off both my part-ner and me and organizing many aspects of our business so that we weren't chasing our tails unnecessarily.

Two years later, I received a call from a woman I had worked with at a former job, and she was interested in whether or not we had any part-time secretarial work. I remembered her as a very able, articulate, knowledgeable person who would be an asset to any business, so I arranged an interview with my partner and myself. In between, we got a notice from our administrator that he was leaving because he felt two part-time jobs were beginning to get to him—he needed to consolidate. We were still not in a position to offer him a full-time job, and he had had an offer elsewhere that sounded ap-pealing to him. So we included him in the interview with the woman who had called, and the two of them made such a smooth and fluid transition of his leaving and her moving into his job that the business was able to roll on without the disastrous effect we had expected with the loss of our friend.

The actual formation of the Institute itself was the result of a series of accidents and coincidences. My partner and I had previously been involved with another organization in which we had many differences with the administration. We tried every conceivable way we could think of to work them out, but nothing worked. Finally, we both resigned, totally depressed and despairing. At that point, a friend suggested to my partner that we start our own place and even went so far as to outline just what we would need and how much it would cost. My partner called me, said he wanted me to do this with him, but would do it even if he had to manage it alone. I was frightened of the idea, but my husband pushed me to do it and was very willing to contribute to the financial investment which my partner and I would have to make at the start. As it turned out, of course, it was one of the best investments either of us ever made in terms of our growth on every level, and it was certainly far superior in the range of opportunities it has offered to us than what we left.

I have learned that on an energy level there is no wasted motion. Every experience results in learning without effort—all is useful in terms of growth to everyone involved; every event holds within it the seed for expansion, knowledge, increased awareness, or joy of living, which is the most productive growth experience there is. All one needs to do is to pay attention to what external events and coincidences might be telling him and not get hooked on a particular end product or conclusion. I have learned that I can determine what I want, but I cannot program the way in which it comes about, the timing, or who is involved in bringing it about. I have to let go and trust my own intuitive processes to bring it about in the way and place that is most perfect in time for me and everyone else involved.

In the instance I mentioned earlier, about my friend and the mansion that was her dream house, her ability to stay with that dream—but let go of hanging on to a particular form of that dream—enabled her to see that house as a beacon rather than a loss.

When you begin to consider dreams as real events actually occuring on another level of consciousness, then your dreams will become increasingly clear and readable in terms of your overall process. It is as though the loosening of controls makes it unnecessary for your other levels of consciousness to mask what is going on. For example, a woman I know had been struggling with whether or not she wanted to get her face lifted. She knew that the result would be pleasing to her, and she knew a doctor she trusted, but she was afraid of the idea of surgery. One night she had a dream in which she went through the whole operation successfully and was totally pleased at the outcome. She was even able to recall specific aspects of the surgery and her experience afterward. When she was telling me about the dream, she indicated that she saw it as precognitive—a preview of an event that had already occurred. But it would come about on her time span, and she felt her insides revealed the data to her to reassure and encourage her.

In another instance, a client of mine was debating whether or not she would break up with a man she had been seeing. She had a dream in which she saw him enjoying himself with another woman. She immediately felt relieved because she realized he could be happy with someone else, and she wasn't doing him any favor by dragging things out.

Another client had a violent outburst with her five year old child which really frightened her. When she told me about it, I indicated to her that I thought her child was triggering rage that really belonged to her own experience as a five-year-old and that maybe we could now begin to deal with that. She then had a dream in which she expressed rage at a father who had deserted her. Further in the dream she saw her husband. At first he was lying in a casket at his own funeral; then he was alive and laughing with her. She felt that his role as a kind of surrogate father to her was dead and that she and he were now ready to connect as two adults who didn't need to make up to each other for parental loss. She felt that her ability to begin to take charge of her own rage and sadness and to deal with them openly without feeling guilty made it possible to break the old bonds.

Often I will have dreams that will validate what I am doing on a conscious level. It is as though some other part of me is saying "Yes, you're doing what fits for you—all is in harmony." Sometimes they offer me clues about other directions I hadn't considered consciously. For example, I had been angry with someone whom I felt was really depreciating in her behavior towards me. I had a dream in which she and I were walking together and she was very depressed and angry. I remember being surprised at the intensity of her feeling because it was so different from her usually calm, unpertrubed demeanor. I then realized on waking up that she was at a stage in her growth in which she was experiencing sadness and anger periodically because she was at a place where she needed to make a major change and it was difficult for her. Therefore, her unpredictable behavior of moving toward me and then moving away was not intended as an affront to me. It was a statement that at times she could be with others, and at times she had to take space to deal with her own feelings. That knowledge didn't make me feel less angry because I wanted her to be able to tell me that clearly and not leave me in the dark. However, it did enable me to be more charitable toward her and to stop making life difficult for myself.

It isn't my intent to encourage you to obsess over everything that happens to you until you figure it out. What I am encouraging is for you to open yourself up to whatever meaning may be in every experience. If no answer comes, simply file the data away on your insides and trust that answers will come at the best time, when it is most fitting and you are ready. In this process, we must learn to move without knowing all the answers, trusting our intuitive processes to reveal what we need to know when we need to know it.

19
Relationships in the Energy Framework

"WHEN YOU CAN LOVE A PERSON only if she or he is able to act in a fashion that fits your addictive programming, you are treating the other person as an object to be manipulated."*

Relationships are often based on need rather than a desire for sharing and exploration. We need someone to validate us, to assuage our pain or loneliness, to make us feel whole. As long as we fulfill each others' expectations in that respect, we are able to give and express love. However, if the other person functions in such a way that his or her partner feels insecure, unappreciated or uncertain, love is withdrawn. For example, a husband and wife have had a connection in which he was the "strong" one—he made the decisions, established the rules, provided for the family. She took care of him—provided the meals, a clean house, sex, clean clothes, and the management of the children—in return for having someone to lean on and take responsibility for major decisions as well as the welfare of the family. That arrangement may work very well for both of them, and their love for each other may be based on the maintenance of that arrangement. If, however, the wife's growth takes her in the direction of making more decisions for herself, taking more assertive action and responsibility, the husband may see that as a depreciation of him and as her lack of respect for his expertise as a provider. He becomes critical, judgmental, and withdraws love and affection.

On the other hand, perhaps the husband's growth takes him in the direction of paying more attention to his own feelings which makes him seem less reliable and dependable to his wife. He opts to go fishing rather than build the shelves she wants. He decides not to go to a party she wants to attend. He begins to talk openly about

---

*Ken Keyes, Jr., *Handbook to Higher Consciousness.* Berkeley: Living Love Center.

what he considers his weaknesses, inadequacies, uncertainties. His wife feels betrayed, disappointed, afraid. She withdraws her respect which was based on his adherence to an image rather than his identity as a person. She feels justified in viciously depreciating him because, after all, he has let her down. This is the kind of possessive, dictatorial, inhibiting connection that we have often accepted as a love, friendship, family relationship. In Henry James' story of "Daisy Miller" (now a movie), the writer presents a graphic picture of the ultimate structure for the death of aliveness—Victorian society. Daisy could only go far enough in her pursuit of life to appear insipid, scatterbrained and rebellious; not far enough to take an assertive stand for life and her own identity. Her admirer, Mr. Winterborn, responded to her aliveness but could not validate his response by active pursuit of her because she did not conform to the expectations of her day—the very thing that would have squelched the quality he loved. How often we use love as the sop in exchange for giving up charge of ourselves. How often is love the mask for control—if you love me, you will . . . if I love you, I will . . .

How often do we give—and buy—the depreciating message, "I could love you more if you would only change—." In therapy sessions, I have often said to a husband and wife, "Consider that each of you is giving all that is fitting for you to give and is not withholding out of lack of love or stubborn rebellion. You are simply being who you are to the best of your ability. If you accepted that, how would you feel about each other?" If you cannot look at your partner and say, "I accept you exactly the way you are," then much of your relationship will mask a power struggle—an attempt to use the promise of love as a seductive weapon to induce the other person to change to better satisfy your expectations.

When an individual is connected to his intuitive processes and his sense of himself as an energy system for his survival and aliveness, he does not need to control someone else. He may love someone and choose not to be around that person on a concrete level because their relationship is not satisfying or enhancing to both of them, but he will be able to let go and trust his intuitive self to attract into his orbit the persons most fitting to his current evolutionary state. When an individual genuinely believes that his expanded levels of consciousness will protect him from harm, then he can open himself to whatever experience occurs and savor that experience to the fullest. If he also believes that he creates his own world and that his insides create the forms into which other people and events fit, then he doesn't need defenses. We often play all kinds of games to keep others from knowing how we really feel, to make sure we can reject before we get rejected, to keep ourselves from looking awkward, making a mistake, or looking foolish. All of those facades take considerable energy to maintain and prevent us from making real contact with each other. We are like fighters in a ring, dancing around, sizing each other up, waiting for the other to make the first move so that we don't have to risk. As a result, we become reactors responding to stimuli rather than asserting from our own inner aliveness. Reactors are natural victims.

"Sexual communication is a form of soul communion ... When this is the case there is a flow of vital forces from one to the other, enhancing the awareness of life and resulting in an uplift of consciousness."* When two individuals trust their insides totally, then all energy can go into a couple letting go into the experience with each other without fear of harm or loss. As that happens, data begins to flood in from all levels of consciousness.

For example, I can be having dinner with a man with whom I am involved. We can be carrying on a casual conversation over dinner. At the same time, I may be aware of two people (still us) having a whole other conversation on another level of consciousness. That level of communication does not have a back and forth framework. Communication is mutual and instantaneous. "In consciousness (thoughts and emotions) communication is instantaneous ... You operate as if your thoughts were secret, though you should know by now that they are not. Not only are your thoughts apparent through telepathic communications ... but they also form pseudo-images beneath the range of physical matter as you normally perceive it ..."*

As we are having dinner, perhaps we are discussing the concert we have just attended. I am feeling warm and affectionate as a result of the energy flowing between and within each of us. We are, in essence, touching each other on a consciousness level quite separate

*Roy Eugene Davis, *The Way of the Initiate*. CSA Press, 1970.
*Roberts, *Seth Speaks*.

from the words we are saying. Behaviorally, we are lifting knives and forks in the ritual of eating. On a consciousness level, we are loving and touching each other. Suddenly, I feel a withdrawal as though we are distant even though our conversation and behavior appear the same. I initially attribute the withdrawal to him, but then I realize that experience on a consciousness level is mutual, and I recognize that both of us are a little afraid. At that point, one of us may decide to raise that level of communication to the concrete, verbal, cognitive area of awareness. If we can do that and both accept and relate to that data without feeling blame or distrusting ourselves, then the relationship will intensify and progress because there is a developing balance among all levels of consciousness. If one of us denies that data or feels attacked or insecure in the face of it, the relationship will falter or become increasingly rocky.

In addition to being aware of the concrete exchange and the intuitive consciousness communication, we may also be experiencing deja vu phenomena. I may suddenly see the other person or both of us in another place, another time, even in other forms of dress. "Deep relationships will continue in one way or another. Others will simply disappear."* Perhaps our connection goes beyond the concrete experience of this lifetime. Perhaps we are finishing something or expanding something that we began in another time or place. How often have you met people whom you felt you have always known? It is entirely possible that you *have* always known that person on a consciousness level and that your mutual energy systems are old friends. If that is so and if we open our minds to that possibility, then I believe that we will increasingly get data about other aspects of our connections.

As you can see, all of this is a great deal of data to handle and requires that each of us have a strong sense of identity so that we can assimilate it and respond to it without losing balance. "It is theoretically possible for any of you to disperse your consciousness and become a part of any object in the room—or to fly apart, to disperse yourself out into space—without leaving your sense of identity."* In a deeply intimate relationship, without defense, you ex-

*Roberts, *Seth Speaks.*
*Ibid.

perience that kind of merging of consciousness. You literally become part of each other without any loss of self—on the contrary, your awareness of yourself is heightened by the contact. "Males and females need each other . . . For the positive-negative electrical interchange resulting from close proximity . . ."*

It is possible that an individual can connect with someone else via their expanded levels of consciousness, but not concretely. Have you ever had the experience of feeling a flow of energy, a heightened awareness between you and another person, but the other person denies that feeling? Or have you had a relationship in which you experienced deep moments of tenderness and intimacy only to have the other person behave later as though that exchange of feeling or that depth had never occurred? Many times the expanded levels of awareness operate without connection to the cognitive level. The individual does not allow himself to recognize those feelings. The feelings on that level are so powerful that he cannot own them without fear of losing control. Again, the ability to handle the intensity we are capable of feeling requires a solid sense of identity. Otherwise, on a deep level of consciousness we fear being lost, overwhelmed, swallowed up. Therefore, we will seek out relationships in which we can maintain control—either because our feelings are not strong enough to bind us to the other person (we can always walk away if things get too threatening), or the other person is dependent on us. Either way, we can then maintain the relationship without having to get in touch with and assert feelings that we perceive as too powerful to handle. The price we pay for such stability is to dilute or deaden our experience of our own aliveness.

When the individual's sense of identity is strong enough to allow him to trust his intuitive processes completely, he can allow himself to be totally carried away by his feelings because he trusts his insides to protect him and lead him in a more positive direction. In that instance, the basis of the relationship is primarily on the intuitive level, and the concrete level of connection is utilized only for nurturance. Verbally and behaviorally, each gives the other approval, validation, and physical contact for the purpose of nourishing and expanding the intuitive levels of consciousness. All real communica-

---

*Davis, *Way of the Initiate*.

tion and learning then occurs increasingly on the intuitive level of their connection. As they express to each other what they experience intuitively in terms of feelings, images, fantasies, dreams, sensations, they use the concrete level to check out, explore, and further define their perceptions. That process deepens awareness and sharpens their perceptual ability with each other.

The ability to experience intimacy on this level, without addiction, grounds the individual in this world. Such relationships induce the deepest kind of commitment based on a level of mutual awareness and trust that goes far beyond any cognitive concepts of duty or responsibility. The pleasure in such relationships is intense, ever-expanding and lasting. Such a depth of experience is necessary if one is to go into the exploration of expanded levels of consciousness because that level is so seductive that it would draw an individual totally away from this world if he did not have an equally strong pull in this direction. Without this balance, I think we would go off on a mountain top or simply leave this world altogether. I feel that the grounding here is vital in terms of our own evolution and the evolution of the race. In my judgment, we are at a place for the first time in our history where it is possible to move into this arena of exploration from a balanced position. Always before, people have moved into this level without intellectual understanding, cultural support, sense of self-worth and security, and sensual awareness. As a result, they have been ostracized as witches or mental cases, set apart as gods; or they have burned themselves out or isolated themselves in monasteries.

I think the primary source of grounding is the intimate relationship. However, I feel that sensuality on all levels is also vital in such grounding. It is important to enjoy good food, wine, beauty, air, scenery, exercise—whatever turns you on physically, but without addiction. If the individual can totally let go into his sensuality without having to hang on to the person, places, or objects involved, then he is free to be totally alive in the moment without fear of loss or harm. Thus, all energy is involved in the total experience of aliveness based on rhythm and flow. The sensual area then becomes the experimental arena for testing out and exploring the data garnered from the expanded levels of consciousness. He can utilize his relationships to expand his knowledge and use of his fantasies, dreams, sensations, and images. He can utilize his expanded consciousness for greater perception and enjoyment of the world around him. His ability to move back and forth between the concrete and the ephemeral level provides him with a stabilizing balance and an experimental arena until he is one with all energy around him—animate and inanimate, matter and spirit. Thus, his shift from a concrete base into pure energy is gradual. The natural progression of life is not jolting—that is why death as we know it is unnatural. The natural progression of life is flowing, easy—a soft, warm, airy, velvet passageway.

20
Another Journey Begins...

"We are on the verge of the new age, a whole new world,
Mankind's consciousness, our mutual awareness, is going
to make a quantum leap. Everything will change. You will
never be the same. All this will happen just as soon as
you're ready."*

AS I HAVE BEEN WRITING THIS BOOK, I have been aware that the experience marks the letting go of one way of being and the beginning
of another. I have learned all I need to learn by the avenue of suffering. I must now find another way. I feel as though one life is over
and another beginning. Perhaps that is the way it is as we evolve.
All lives, all aspects of life, become conscious and connected to each
other and we awaken as one and yet many, all at the same time.

---

*Williams, *Das Energi*

Bibliography

[1] Ernest Holmes,, *The Science of Mind.* Dodd Mead and Co., 1938.

[2] Ambrose A. Worrall with Olga N. Worrall, *The Gift of Healing.* Harper and Row, 1965.

[3] Harmon H. Bro, Ph.D., *Edgar Cayce on Religion and Psychic Experience.* New York: © Warner Books.

[4] Ibid.

[5] Jo Anne Chase, as told to Constance Moon, *You Can Change Your Life Through Psychic Power.* New York: Pocket Cardinal Edition.

[6] Buckminster Fuller in a lecture at San Jose State College.

[7] Ostrander and Schroeder, *Psychic Discoveries.*

[8] Bach, Richard, *Jonathon Livingston Seagull.* ©1970.

[9] Holmes, *Science of Mind.*

[10] Ibid.

[11] Russell Paul Schofield, "Actualism—The Actual Design of Man as a Cosmic Being." From *Maps of Consciousness* by Ralph Metzner. 1971.

[12] Alice A. Bailey, "Esoteric Astrology." New York: Lucis Publishing Co., 1981, p. 16.

[13] Ralph Metzner, *Maps of Consciousness.*

[14] Holmes, *Science of Mind.*

[15] Elmer Green, "Biofeedback for Mind-Body Self-Regulation: Healing and Creativity." *The Varieties of Healing Experience*—Transcript of the Interdisciplinary Symposium, October 30, 1971.

[16] Roberts, *Seth Speaks.*

[17] Ambrose A. Worrall and Olga N. Worrall, *Explore Your Psychic World.* Harper and Row, 1970.

[18] Holmes, *Science of Mind.*

[19] Ibid.

[20] Jack H. Holland, Ph.D., "Parapsychology and Medicine in Perspective." *Varieties of Healing Experience.*

[21] Roberts,*Seth Speaks.*

[22] Ibid.

[23] Ibid.

[24] "The Importance of Biological Clocks in Mental Health," *National Institute of Mental Health Reports,* 1968, #2.

[25] Worral and Worral, *Explore Your Psychic World.*

[26] Ostrander and Schroeder, *Psychic Discoveries.*

[27] Ibid.

[28] Shafica Karagulla, "Breakthrough to Creativity." Marina Del Rey, Calif: De Vorss, 1967.